9II

Urgent
Dating Solutions

911

Urgent Dating Solutions

By

Gail Burgess, RN
The Dating Advice Nurse

Cover design by Frederic Tiberghien

Social Lite Productions
Rancho Santa Margarita, CA

Updated September 1999

ISBN: 0-9668983-0-3
Published by: Social Lite Productions
                 31441 Santa Margarita Pkwy. Suite A 359
                 Rancho Santa Margarita, CA 92688

Book cover design by Frederic Tiberghien
Typesetting and layout by Victoria Graphics

Printed in the United States of America

This book is dedicated to

Morgan Christopher Hebard

Table of Contents

Acknowledgments

To the following people I wish to offer my sincere gratitude and thanks:

- To my daughter, Andrea: for saving me when I lost things in the computer and didn't know how to retrieve them; and for keeping my perspective joyful with your sense of humor; knowing you is a gift.
- To my son in-law, Chris: if it weren't for your example, I wouldn't have been inspired to undergo this project. I'd also like to thank you for your generosity, advice, and compassion. You've been a secret angel.
- To Dorothy Fortune, the word and phrase wizard: for your altruism, friendship, and assistance, initially editing and coaching me through this book.
- To Barbara Clark: for your recommendation to go it alone.
- To my brother Scott, the financial guru: for helping me with my projections and assisting me through all sorts of financial matters throughout my lifetime, I'm in appreciation of you always.
- To my family: for your loyalty and support. Thank you mom and dad for instilling honesty, hard work, character, and integrity, as the primary values in my life.
- To Betty Otte, my business mentor: for volunteering your time and expertise. You're a living example of what life is about—giving back to others.

- To my co-workers: for their support during this project. There are certain nurses that have been especially helpful.
- To my supportive friends: through your strength and encouragement, I'm able to walk through anything.
- To Shirl Thomas: thank you for your professional writing advice and consultation.
- To Avrom Lefkowitz, M.F.C.C.: thank you for your advice on relationships and your help with this writing project.
- To my dog, Perry: thank you for making me takes walks when I didn't want to.
- To God.

Introduction

Sitting on the couch, on a Saturday night, with nothing to do and nowhere to go, constitutes a real-life emergency (911!) Especially if that this routine has crept upon you as a way of life. When in such a position, all you can think about is, "Why does everyone else in the world have someone to love, and I don't? When will it be my turn?" A sad and frightening thought. When in this frame of mind, it becomes difficult to come up with creative ideas for dating. So you end up renting yet another home video and eating popcorn on the couch by yourself.

People often believe their soul mates will turn up through the random events of their daily lives. Once in a while they do—but, more often, finding someone with whom to have a relationship, comes from preparing a full, well-planned dating life—just as you'd prepare for a career.

Who would have thought you'd end up in this position—single, in a world full of busy strangers? So now you've either got to get out there and find someone to love, or accept the alternative of growing old alone. Since most of us would prefer to have a lifelong companion, we must first get out there and date.

Maybe you've already taken steps toward enhancing your dating life. Maybe you've read The Rules and MEN ARE FROM MARS, Women Are from Venus. Most of us know all about "how to have a relationship." But where in the world do we go and what do we do to get the dates so that we can have a relationship? I'll show you how.

When you need a lawyer, a stockbroker, or a physician, you call someone with training and success in the field. In seeking help for dating endeavors, again you'd look for someone with credibility. My experience would be warrant a Doctorate in Dating—if such a degree existed—based on ten years of dating all sorts of people from varied backgrounds and professions.

I am unique in that I've organized and shared the lessons and conclusions I've gained from meeting people. My methodical nature, training as a patient educator, and background in marketing and public relations, have contributed to the outcome of this endeavor. Party planning events and fund-raising ventures, have given me the experience and knowledge it takes, to help others learn to have a rich and fulfilling dating life.

Through the years, I've honed and developed a full and extensive social life, encompassing; sports; fund-raising activities; singles events; political activities; parties; contributing time and effort to community groups; singing; acting; and performing as a stand-up comic. Many dates have developed through these and other endeavors, giving me a wealth of experience regarding what to do and what not to do.

I understand how to be a "magnet for meeting people," and can teach you likewise. Other nurses at my work have come to regard me as their "social director" for dating.

Because I've enjoyed, delighted in, and have felt content while dating through the years, I know I can help you become a master at meeting and attracting a companion. Whether you want a lifetime mate or simply a fulfilling relationship, I'll assist you in finding the man or the woman that's right for you. Even if you're shy or haven't been on the dating scene for awhile, this book will help you to get into the game.

The secret to attracting a mate and securing dates is in maintaining an attitude that results in a positive stance. You'll learn to have the ability to take this position whenever you leave your house. When you follow two basic steps: planning and action, you'll meet someone special. The sooner you're willing to take these steps, the sooner you'll be dating.

That's why this book is different. I give you the map to follow to find many people to date, as often as you'd like. By reading and following the suggestions in this book you'll find out how to plan for the days, the weeks, and the months ahead—during which time you'll be dating and **will meet someone to love.**

You'll be able to kiss loneliness good-bye, because you'll know how to plan your social life! Remember that dating is a numbers game. The more times you try, the sooner you'll have what you want, and rightly deserve, because you did the work. By following your new plan, I promise **YOU WILL BE DATING.**

Getting Started

Therapeutic attitudes

Prepare to perform

Congratulations, by picking up this book, you've taken the first step for improving your social life and meeting someone special. Making the decision to do whatever it takes, for as long as it takes, is the key to finding a mate. By making that decision right now, you're a success!

Many dead ends and bumpy roads often accompany a quest for the right person. Some strange and unusual people may cross your path. I say this as a reminder of the realities of socializing and strongly urge you to keep a sense of humor while embarking on this adventuresome journey.

Planning your personal life is similar to running a business. One needs an accounting department to pay bills and allot for spending money. Management and personnel departments for scheduling work each day and acting in a responsible manner. You're your own boss! While running this business, you wouldn't neglect the marketing department, would you?

The marketing department is designed to advertise the business. How are you doing in this department? What sorts of actions are you taking to promote yourself to find a possible mate? Do people know you're available for dating?

Implement the marketing department by following the suggestions in this book, and I guarantee you'll be able to meet the man or woman you've been waiting for.

One of the reasons people fail at finding a dating companion is in presuming that someone will appear at random, not so. Successful encounters take planning, action, and perseverance. Sometimes people do meet unexpectedly, but it's usually because of a mutual friend, sport, or undertaking. By following my proven methods, you'll embark on an eventful social life and **WILL BE DATING**.

I suggest people choose the right activities for their individual needs based on physical, mental, emotional, and monetary means.

Let's begin

As you read through the chapters of this book, highlight places of most interest to you. Note or mark the attitudes and actions you feel willing to take.

Create a monthly calendar to schedule commitment activities and random activities. After reading each chapter, determine which will serve as commitments and which will be allocated as random. Attend commitment activities regularly, making them a part of your routine, keeping random activities as options. See the next few pages for examples.

Decide upon the frequency of your outings. Remember that the more time spent socializing, the sooner someone to love will materialize. Three times a week is a good beginning.

On the next page is a list, followed by a sample calendar. Place an asterisk (*) next to the commitment activities; place a pound (#) sign next to the activities that will be random.

- Some possible <u>Commitment</u> activities:
    1. Gym—three times a week
    2. Coffeehouse—once a week
    3. Church—once a week
    4. Computer graphics class—once a week
    5. Chamber of Commerce mixer— once a month
    6. Answer singles ads—once a week
    7. Place singles ads—once a month
    8. Cultural event—once a month

- Some possible <u>Random</u> activities:
    1. City Council meetings
    2. Singles dances
    3. Sierra Club hiking group
    4. Nightclubs
    5. An appointment with dating services
    6. Singles group activities
    7. Sporting events
    8. Beach or skiing (seasonal outings)

- Write down an activity for each day of the week. Participation is a choice; the point is never having a day without anything to do.
- Answer dating ads once a week, and place ads once a month. This will have you dating in between other activities throughout the week.
- Fill in the calendar at the beginning of each month and keep it out for daily and/or weekly revisions.

Sun.	Mon.	Tues.	Wed.	Thur.	Fri.	Sat.
Church & singles brunch*	Coffee house # Gym*	Computer graphics class*	Gym* *Dating workshop	Chamber of Comm. mixer#	Appt. @ dating service #	Line dancing lessons*
Church & singles brunch*	Coffee house # Gym*	Computer graphics class*	Gym* *Dating workshop	Place singles ad	Singles dinner #	Party at a friends house
Church & singles brunch*	Coffee house # Gym*	Computer graphics class*	Gym* *Dating workshop	Answer singles ad	Answer internet ads #	Nightclub*
Church & singles brunch*	Coffee house # Gym*	Computer graphics class*	Gym* *Dating workshop	Singles hiking group #	Spectator sport #	Bowling with group*
Church & singles brunch*	Coffee house # Gym*	Computer graphics class*	Gym* *Dating workshop	Political meeting #	Karaoke with group #	Beach party #

- Reevaluate the proposed schedule of activities. If the outings haven't resulted in getting dates, realize it's merely an adjustment problem and reorganize the excursions on your calendar. Perhaps you'll want to switch activities that aren't allowing you to meet others frequently. Maybe the time, or day of the week is the problem. Experiment with these elemental issues by adjusting them. Remain persistent; keep an upbeat outlook; think creatively; and be bold. These are other variants to success in the dating arena.

- After reading the book, come back to this chapter, Getting Started, as a reference for filling out your social schedule each month.

- Reread this book as needed for inspiration and motivation. Earmark the pages that provide the boost you need to continue the search for that special someone.

- Now it's time to explore the choices . . . seventeen sections follow. You'll learn where to go and the attitudes to take when at any event. I'll provide a list of places to meet people, and what to do once you're there. Furthermore, you'll learn tips apropos to dating and how to break the ice. We'll look at case studies to illustrate how the methods work. Resources for further encouragement, and references for finding activities of any sort, are provided. Lastly, blank calendars are furnished at the end of the book which you'll fill out for the beginning of your new social life.

Treatment Plan One

A Vicarious Thrill. . .Spectator sports and games

Spectator Sports

This chapter has more of an edge for women to meet men, other chapters lean more toward advantages for men to meet women. However, all of the chapters are helpful for both genders regarding where to go and what to do. Each chapter includes spiritual, emotional, mental, and physical elements to help you meet people.

Therapeutic attitudes

Meet people wherever you go

When thinking about dating we may tend to consider only a few areas for meeting people such as, through friends, singles dances, or bar-hopping. All are valid venues for meeting, but there are far more places to go and ways to meet than those common and familiar arenas. Spectator sports are one of them.

General opinion is men attend spectator sports to watch

the games, not to get dates. In fact, however, while perhaps not consciously looking for dates, most men are looking all the time. With this in mind, know that someone to date could be right there in the stands. All kinds of spectator sports are gold mines for meeting men.

At most events, milling around is quite acceptable. When my girlfriends and I go to baseball games, we first find our seats, then check out the men seated nearby. If nobody looks interesting, we get up and start mingling.

The first area we consider is the most expensive seating section, because we prefer the over thirty, white-collar types who are most likely in the area. Of course, each individual would seek his or her preference. If we see men with appeal, we find seats near them and sit down. Of course when the stands are too full, or the ushers too strict, this move doesn't work. In that case, we head straight to the concession stands to check out the guys.

One needn't look like a movie star to meet men or women. We all know individuals who aren't very attractive; but, because they're outgoing and interested in others, we feel comfortable around them and their physical traits aren't an issue of concern.

The key to making connections anywhere, including spectator-sporting events, is a willingness to strike up a conversation. One way to start is with a funny comment or question. While in line at the concession stand you could ask questions such as, "This is a gourmet hot dog stand isn't it? Where do they keep the Grey Poupon Dijon?" or "Have you ever heard of anyone dying from eating too many hot dogs? This is my third one today."

While seated, you could ask, "Who's the player that just

stepped up to the plate? Is that Babe Ruth?" Most men can't resist responding to a funny or dumb comment, especially if they can correct you for not knowing their heroes. It would be as if a man asked a woman if she were going to lose weight by attending Nutrasweet or Jenny Jones, instead of Nutrasystem and Jenny Craig. Duh!

I'll not offer commonplace advice such as, "be confident," "be strong," or "don't be nervous." Yet those are the exact psychological conditions needed to get out and meet people. Instead of attempting to live up to trite suggestions that might go against your basic personality, try acting, masquerading, or pretending you're the person you'd like to be.

People have a tendency toward this playacting anyway, on days that aren't going particularly well. Being polite to the checkout clerk at the grocery store, smiling, or saying hello to our colleagues at work is a form of acting if, at the time, we'd really rather ignore them.

Think of it as your "job" to attend a spectator sport. Pretend, for example, that you're a reporter for a newspaper, covering a news story. Imagine the spectators are there to help you learn about the game, the players, and the teams. Ask for their opinions on the sport and the athletes. Find out how often they attend the games. Ask, as many questions as you can think of—keeping in mind their responses will be featured in your imaginary news column.

If you tend to be nervous in crowds, smile. Pretend you're a model or a politician, having to smile at everyone and everything all of the time. Put on one of those "mannequin like" smiles. I swear it works. After awhile, you tend to become happy even if you're riddled with anxiety. Make a game of it, by keeping a mental note of how many men or women say "hello," in response to a smile. Notice how many follow you back to your seat or to the concession stand.

Whether at a hockey game or merely taking a walk, when you know you're the owner and creator of the attitude toward your experiences, you can take charge of your life by deciding to have a good time with others. Repeat affirmations such as, "I choose to participate fully in everything I do; by thinking kind thoughts; talking with all sorts of people; and creating my own fun."

For Women

When surveying "mankind," I'm assuming you're with a friend and are capable of defending yourself, not tolerating a drunkard or someone who seems mentally unstable or vulgar. Quickly distance yourself from anyone of that nature. If you live in a high crime area or are going to a dense city, carry pepper spray or take a self-defense class.

Don't harm yourself by wasting your precious time on anyone who's likely to make you unhappy. Setting standards in the beginning is the secret to selecting a worthy mate.

Prescription for where to go

Check your vicinity for spectator sports or games such as:
- Air shows: airplanes, helicopters, and jets
- Baseball: major or minor league, college, or amateur games
- Basketball: The National Basketball Association games, amateur, or college games

- Bowling: professional tours or amateur competitions
- Boxing events: professional, amateur, or college
- Equestrian events: riding, polo, or rodeos
- Football: The National Football League games, amateur, or college games
- Golf: The Professional Golf Association games, amateur or charity competitions
- Hockey: The National Hockey League games, amateur, or college games
- Horse or Dog races: at horse or dog racing tracks
- Motor sports: auto racing, all-terrain vehicle racing, boat racing, or motorcycle racing
- Soccer: professional games, college, or amateur games
- Tennis: The United States Tennis Association, amateur, college, or charity tournaments or games
- Volleyball: professional tours, college, or amateur events
- Wrestling: college, amateur, or professional events

Cures for what to do

Be friendly and casual when talking to others. Lighten up the spirit of your surroundings by amiably commenting on people or things. For instance, if someone is wearing a baseball cap with an Angels logo on it, you could say "Nice cap. Are you a guardian angel by any chance?" or "Does that cap mean to say you're an angel? Are you for hire? I could use a guardian angel."

Choose a couple of people in the seats around you to warm up to as if you were old friends. Ask them questions or inquire as to their opinion of the game. Being amongst others, supporting your team, cheering players on, talking with others; creates a fun, wholesome atmosphere. When people see exchange of this nature, they want to be part of the fun too. Relating mutually with each other strikes a cord in everyone at a deep level, so much so, that you can get a crowd of eight to ten people chumming with each other during a game.

Becoming friendly and bold in taking the chance to have fun and laugh with others is power. It takes courage to go beyond any fear of strangers and then interact. One of the many definitions of happiness is to find a fear and conquer it. Succeeding at having a good time at an event, and investing in your social life with the possibility of getting a date, is certainly conquering a fear. The more practice you have at interacting with others, the more secure you become. When you do this, you begin to attract others who are powerful too. You'll get the attention of those who also know how to enjoy life. The more you practice self-expression, the better you become at the art of socializing.

"Laughter is the best medicine," is often true. Having fun, talking, and being silly are as essential as eating fruits, vegetables, and taking multivitamins. Without a light mixture, you're sentenced to a life of cruel and unusual punishment.

<u>For Men</u>

Ask a woman out for coffee or a drink right after the game. If she's unable to accompany you at the time, ask for her phone number. This might sound simplistic, but people forget about asking for dates when they go to places other than nightclubs or bars. <u>Ask women out wherever you go.</u>

For Women

I hope you want to say "yes," but if not, make sure you know how to say "no." If a man asks you out or requests your phone number and you aren't interested, say, "Thanks, but I'm not available." They need to know nothing more about you or your situation. You need not give a long-winded explanation. I can't tell you how many men would rather hear the truth outright, in the beginning, than have to play guessing games and phone tag.

First-aid procedures for breaking the ice

Wear something that makes a statement or invites conversation. An example would be a descriptive piece of jewelry, such as a golf pendant, or a cute animal. Be seen in a cap bearing a logo or printing on it, or sport suspenders adorned with a remarkable design.

Wearing unusual articles of clothing or jewelry, gives people an opportunity to comment about its uniqueness. It may be the cue that someone needed to talk to you, but wouldn't have known what to say otherwise.

In the same vein, look for people wearing unusual clothing or holding items like programs or banners. Ask where they got them—comment on them. This is your opener. From there, ask questions such as, "Where are you sitting?" "What are you doing after the game?" "Do you live in the area?" "Do come to these events often?" "Do you hold tickets for the season?" "Do you know any of the players?" and so forth.

Remedies and tips

While your hope is to meet someone to date and find somebody to love, you shouldn't make it your only reason for being there. If Mr. or Ms. Right, or even Mr. or Ms. So-So, doesn't come along, you'll be disappointed unless you come to regard your social life as a journey that gives you a plethora of life experiences in which to take pleasure from.

Enjoying your life is an end in itself. You're making progress the moment you leave your house to do something different. You'll begin to create an air about you that you wouldn't have had if you spent time alone watching cooking shows on TV, or even worse, testing those recipes and eating them all by yourself. Or, sticking your nose to the boob tube for endless hours of watching football or movies, and then wondering where the time went.

Sometimes spending too much time alone creates a downward spiral of energy, which can send you into a slump of isolation, which begets depression. By going out, moving your body, and doing something different, you come alive. Move it or lose it is where this expression comes in to play.

Case studies

One day my friend Diane and I met two good-looking men at an Angel's game. Diane is a cute, petite, blonde dietician, who resembles Lady Di. We wanted to meet some men, so off to a baseball game we went. We knew men congregated at baseball stadiums, and did they ever! The place was loaded with them: small ones, tall ones, old ones, young ones, handsome ones, and homely ones—all kinds of men. The odds were about eight men to one woman . . . paradise!

We flirted by smiling at a couple of men in the concession stand while waiting to order refreshments. Picture a couple of vulnerable, shy and yet sincere teenagers, and you can imagine how we behaved. We smiled and giggled. We'd look at them, smile, and look away; then we'd do it again. Being cute works when it comes to meeting men and besides, it's fun. The men couldn't resist our coy flirtations and, it just so happened, they were seated in the aisle across from us. They waved and motioned for us to sit with them. We gestured that they sit with us, and they moved over.

Afterwards, we went for coffee at a nearby restaurant. My date, Mike, was a tall, blonde bodybuilder and sports equipment salesman from Florida. I immediately recognized we were a geographical impossibility, but we had a good time talking and joking together.

Diane's date, Bill, a medium built and handsome man, turned out to be an emergency room doctor from California. They dated for awhile, until it became apparent he wasn't the right match for Diane.

Although neither of us came away with our lifelong partners— that day at the Angels game was one of the most fun times I've had with Diane.

* * *

My vivacious, redheaded attorney friend, Eileen, and I went to another Angel's game. We followed the same routine

15

as I mentioned previously, checking the seating over for any good looking guys and milling around the season ticket holder's section, then on to the concession stands. We struck out that night, but luckily the Angels didn't.

We shrugged it off to "the girl's night out" and made the best of it by laughing and watching the game. Sitting outdoors and breathing fresh air in the evening at dusk resulted in a wonderful way to spend an evening.

Later, we encountered some likeable men in the restaurant across the street—no one we wanted to date, but were delighted at the attention nonetheless.

Neither Diane, Eileen, nor I held expectations of meeting the "special man" when we attended the ball games. We knew the point was to enjoy the outdoors with each other in the company of men, watching the game, shouting, "Kill the umpire!" and laughing. For the more one enjoys life, the better able to share that joy, humor, and silliness with others and maybe one day . . . fall in love.

Research and development for finding a spectator sport

The Internet

For a listing of various sporting events, type: http://www.sport-hq.com/America's Sports H.Q.: "the Web's sports directory." When you reach that site, highlight the sport of your interest. Schedules of events, as well as local and national addresses and phone numbers are listed. It has a listing of more sports than you have time to watch or play.

Another way to find spectator sports is to surf the Web, one of the following ways:

1) Type in the name of the sport such as bowling, then the name of your city or general vicinity in quotation marks such as: "bowling tournaments" "Los Angeles." The quotation marks tell the computer to be specific in the search, reducing the searched for information to bowling tournaments in Los Angeles.

2) Randomly type an address such as http://www. volleyball.com and see what comes up.

Ticket outlets are another source on the Internet such as *Ticketmaster*. The address is http://www.ticketmaster. com. You'll find their home page at this address.

Or use an Internet directory such as, http://www.four11.com, or http://www.switchboard.com.

Libraries and Bookstores

Libraries check the reference section look for a guide called The Gale Encyclopedia of Associations. Look under the heading of sports, to find a particular sporting association in your area. The contact names, phone numbers, and addresses for the associations are provided.

Or, look in the magazine section for sports magazines.

Bookstores look in the sports, regional, recreation, or entertainment sections of your local bookstore. Certain magazines will focus on a particular sport such as tennis or golf.

Browse for and/or purchase books through the Internet, here are a few sites: http://www.amazon.com, http://

www.bookline.com, http://www.barnesandnoble.com, http:/ /www.bookworld.com, or http://www.borders.com.

Check the Newspaper

The entertainment, life-style, regional, and/or sports sections have listings and advertisements for happenings. Read these sections each day or at least once a week to pursue the events you'd like to attend.

Sometimes free local newspapers are great resources for sports and games.

Utilize the Phone Directory

The Yellow Pages have alphabetical listings by topic. For example, look up the name of a sport such as golf. Find one of the better known golf courses in your area. Call them to ask if they have any amateur games coming up, or if they know when some of the professional tournaments are scheduled to be in town. (The less popular courses may not feature spectator events.)

The White Pages have alphabetical listings by formal names or business names. For example: to find one of the larger golf courses in my area I'd look up the name of the golf course of which I'm familiar, in the "P" section, for Pelican Hill Golf Course.

Some phone directories have separate sections for entertainment, in addition to listings of numerous other events and places of interest, and will contain information on stadiums and stadium seating, along with the phone numbers and addresses of the stadiums.

Sporting Goods and Equipment Stores

Sporting goods stores have events posted on bulletin boards and often times keep flyers on the checkout counters. Big 5 or REI are national chains. Drop by if there's one in your area or call by looking in the Yellow Pages under sporting goods or in the White Pages under Big 5, REI, or another retail outlet with which you're familiar.

Ticket outlets

Look under ticket sales in the Yellow Pages for the spectator sport or interest to you.

The following are sales outlets that supply tickets nationally to major events locally and worldwide, the toll free numbers are:

(800) 422-4002 A Night on the Town ticket agency
(800) 700-8885 Goodtime Tickets
(800) 328-4253 VIP Tickets

Travel Agents

Most of the time travel agents know of spectator sports in regions where you live or to where you'll be traveling. For example, if you were traveling to Georgia, they'd be able to tell you when The Masters Tournament is held in Augusta, and would be able to book your ticket as well. Travel agents are listed in the Yellow Pages under travel or if you know the name of a travel agent, look it up in the White Pages, or on the Internet.

Get Physical … The gym or fitness center

Therapeutic attitudes

<u>Looks aren't everything, but they sure do help</u>

Working out is similar to tuning and lubing your car, keeping it at optimum performance. By moving your joints, taking deep breaths, you increase circulation and oxygenation, while building and toning muscle. This maintains a healthy body and improves your looks in the process. While at it, why not help yourself socially and meet others when you're there?

You may belong to, or have been a member of a gym, but haven't met anyone to date. If you're anything like I've been—the gym was seen as a huge hamster cage for sedentary city-dwellers to exercise. Not a very positive view of fitness centers and gyms—let alone setting up a mental image in preparation for meeting someone. Perhaps you need a new twist on your old way of thinking. Why not take on a new and deliberate perspective on workout facilities, as I've done?

Play a mind game with yourself. Begin thinking of the gym as your possession. Welcome your guests to your workout center by saying "hello" to at least two people each time you're there. In addition, ask others questions such as, "Do you enjoy working out here?" (At my facility.)

By pretending that you own the gym, you assume more control over your environment. It takes you out of a fearful stance, to one of personal power. As the host or hostess of the gym, you must extend yourself to others.

Frame your attitude with the right thoughts before leaving your house for the gym any activity. Repeat an affirmative phrase such as, "Today I'll take care of myself physically. I have confidence in my strong and healthy body. I carry myself well, and in doing so, attract people wherever I go." Even if you don't feel convinced, say it anyway. Someday you'll come to believe it.

Prescription for where to go

Try a gym or fitness center close to your home or office.

Cures for what to do

Single men and women usually exercise before or after work. Typically, anytime between 6 -8 a.m. and 4 -7 p.m. are prime times to go. Experiment with different workout schedules; determine which periods have the majority of single people in your preferred age group. When you decide on the best time for you, stick to it. By becoming a regular, if someone wants to meet you, they'll know the time and day you consistently go.

Develop friendships with same sex acquaintances in order to gather a larger network of friends. You never know who knows whom. For example, while at the gym, I developed a friendship with a policewoman named Nancy. We had much in common, since, at the time, I was an emergency room nurse, and the police frequently came in for traumatic, unusual, or dramatic reasons. Nancy and I would often "talk shop" while working out. Eventually, she invited me to a party where I met two police officers, both of whom I dated on separate occasions.

Another time, marching in true hamster-like fashion on the treadmill, I met Sherry, who exercised on the mouse wheel next to me. I told her how relieved I felt to return to my routine I'd so long neglected. She'd also just returned from a break in her exercise plan. That passing comment led to our working out with each other on Monday and Wednesday mornings, and we became friends.

One of the secrets to obtaining dates is to acquire a network of friends who do things together. Fraternizing with Sherry brought introductions to a few other members; one of whom was the fitness instructor. He'd just completed a photo shoot for a TV commercial and knew lots of exciting people in and outside of the gym . . . a great contact for meeting new people. In addition to his gregarious personality and dynamic life-style, he had the scoop on all of the club members. He knew their ages, marital status, and times they exercised.

Gym members and fitness trainers can be wonderful contacts for your social life. Eventually, you're likely to be invited to parties, outings, and/or events.

For Men

Improvise humorous comments when exercising next to someone with whom you're attracted, by saying something such as, "I'll be on the treadmill for two hours and thirty-five minutes due to the Big Mac attack I had yesterday." Or, "I expect to look like Arnold Schwartzenagger after exercising today. I'm getting close aren't I?" These are only examples; of course you'd say whatever comes to mind in your own way.

If a woman's interested, she'll respond to your comments amiably. If not, you'll receive a brief answer, a smirk, or the cold shoulder. If that's the case, there's no reason to continue talking. Take it in stride and move on.

For Women

Be friendly to everyone, including men with whom you aren't necessarily attracted and also to other women. Even if you don't exactly know what to say, at least smile or give them eye contact as a cordial gesture. Some people feel quite easily rejected, especially if they've taken the chance to talk to a stranger. Do your best to be polite. As others notice your friendliness, you'll be perceived as one who's easily approached, and more opportunities will open up for meeting others.

First-aid procedures for breaking the ice

Wear tee shirts or workout clothes with logos depicting a college, university, or sports team; or some clever slogans such as, *Nothing Changes if Nothing Changes.*

Chris, my son-in-law, has a tee shirt with a picture of a squirrel holding nuts in its cheeks. The picture is a front and side view of the squirrel, as in a mug shot, with a caption reading: Wanted in Four Counties for Robbery. He has another one from the Weekly World News with the picture of a baby with pointy ears and a caption that reads: Bat Child Found in Cave. It's so silly looking, one can't help but laugh. What better way for others to prompt a comment or two?

If, by chance, you notice someone wearing a corny tee shirt or one with a logo on it, initiate an exchange—if only a simple compliment as, "I like your shirt, where did you get it?" As you practice conversing with people, your social-skills and confidence increase.

I recall a time on the rowing machine, mulling over a computer problem I was having, when I noticed a man sitting nearby wearing a tee shirt from The 4th Annual Computer Fairplex. I stopped rowing and approached him to explain my computer problem, asking if he knew how to fix it. As luck would have it, he knew little about computers, but he smiled and gave me that 70's Disco - "Stayin Alive" - John Trivolta kind of look, apparently pleased to be approached by a woman at the gym.

Remedies and tips

Act nonchalant when meeting strangers. The less you appear to take things seriously, the more people will feel relaxed around you.

When we let go of the need to "receive something" such as, attention or a date, and focus on "giving something" as, a greeting or flattering comment, it tends to set people at ease. As we practice giving to others, the more habit-forming it becomes. Wouldn't it be admirable to develop a habit we needn't break?

Getting physically fit is bound to make you more attractive, and the better you look, the more people you'll attract. According to an article by Valerie Frankel, in Mademoiselle magazine, the number-one response from men, when asked what kind of woman they would marry was: attractive. Women want attractive men also. Yet you don't have to be a beautiful woman or a handsome man to be attractive; the definition of attractive is, *the power to attract; pleasing to the eye or mind; charming.* As your body tone develops, you can't help but carry yourself well, which increases confidence . . . causing you to be "pleasing to the eye and mind."

Lastly, since some people have trouble accepting their bodies, I'd like to discuss the three genetic body prototypes, which are:

Ectomorph: illustrative of a slim and narrow body as we see in women such as: Claudia Schiffer or Jane Seymour. With men: a slender, lanky look such as the appearance of James Taylor or Jerry Seinfeld.

Mesomorph: characteristic of the hourglass figure for women such as Jennifer Lopez or Marilyn Monroe. With men: the V-shaped athletic form, similar to Tom Cruise or Mel Gibson.

Endomorph: exemplifying the larger, rounder figure representative of women such as Roseanne Barr or Delta Burke. With men: the round teddy-bear type, such as John Goodman or Elton John.

Many people are a combination of two out of three body types. Accepting your body's form and doing your best to stay toned and active is the healthy thing to do.

In addition, each body type favors particular clothing styles. Determine which clothing styles flatter your body. Choose a couple of good-looking ensembles to use as your "dating uniforms." If you're dating different people, no one will know you're wearing only a few of your most flattering outfits.

Resource

One of the reasons many people have trouble losing or maintaining their weight, even with regular exercise, is diet. Most Americans eat too many refined foods, such as sugar and white flour products. It's important to eat fruits and vegetables. Read *Sugar Busters* by H. Leighton Steward, Morrison C. Bethea, M.D., Sam S. Andrews, M.D., and Luis A. Balart, M.D.; or *The Carbohydrate Addicts Diet* by Rachael F. Heller Ph.D., and Richard F. Heller, Ph.D.; or diet recommendations from the American Diabetes Association. Or, have your doctor give you a referral or some suggestions.

Case Study

Laurie, a bubbly vivacious blonde hairdresser, met her husband Dan at the gym. Dan worked at the gym as a personal fitness trainer and nutritionist. He was attracted to Laurie for months and continually said hello to her. She returned his greeting without much enthusiasm. She thought he was friendly because he wanted to make a sale. Laurie kept to herself when at the gym because it wasn't one of her favorite activities, but rather a "necessary evil."

Dan finally stopped to talk with her. She was surprised when he didn't start in on products or services. It hadn't occurred to her that he was flirting with her for all of those months. He asked her questions and told funny stories, which made her brighten up. She was a pushover for men who could make her laugh.

The very next week, he invited her to dinner. When she asked him why he waited so long to approach, he said he could sense she wasn't ready. He knew timing was everything in relationships, especially with someone as beautiful as she was.

He was right. A few months earlier, she wouldn't have dated him because of a recent breakup with another man.

They became friends, then lovers, and were married a year later. It's been eight years now, and they're doing quite well.

Research and development for finding a gym or fitness center

The Internet

To find a gym or fitness center on the Internet, go to any search vehicle and type in the words: fitness centers, health spas, gymnasiums, or athletic clubs and the name of your town or surrounding cities in quotation marks.

Use http://www.four11.com, http://www.switchboard.

com. These are Internet directories, which are similar to phone books for the Internet.

Utilize the Phone Book

The Yellow Pages list topics or subjects. Check under gymnasiums, fitness centers, health spas, or athletic clubs.

The White Pages list formal names or business names. If you know the gym's name, look it up in the White Pages.

***

– I received a new ad in the mail for a gym. Their mission statement reads: A gym where no one judges you. Then goes on to say, where everyone is made to feel comfortable, regardless of age, width, or unique personal habits. The name of the gym is CRUNCH, located in New York, Miami Beach, Los Angeles, San Francisco, Atlanta, Mission Viejo, Tokyo, and soon to open in Chicago and Las Vegas. Reach them at their Web address: www.crunchfitness.com.

The largest nationwide health club chain in the United States is Bally Total Fitness Health Clubs, with locations in the following states: Arizona, California, Colorado, Connecticut, District of Columbia, Florida, Georgia, Illinois, Indiana, Kansas, Maryland, Massachusetts, Michigan, Minnesota, Missouri, New Jersey, New York, North Carolina, Ohio, Oklahoma, Pennsylvania, Rhode Island, Tennessee, Texas, Utah, Virginia, Washington, and Wisconsin.

To reach Bally Fitness Centers, you may call (800) 348-6377 to find the location nearest you. Or reach their Internet Web page by typing: http://www.ballyfitness.com/home.html.

Colleges

Colleges have gyms in them. Call a local college in your area. Find out if they have a workout center and fitness program. If so, ask them to mail you a program or schedule.

Check things out

When you're driving around town, look for gyms, or ask friends where they go.

Hotels

Hotels have gyms in them. If you travel frequently, you might want to keep this in mind when you're on a business trip or on vacation.

Get Moving . . . Sports teams and/or classes

Therapeutic attitudes

<u>Physical strength increases confidence—bodily and mentally</u>

Taking part in any sport that requires endurance will build physical strength, which truly does increase self-confidence. When you're physically fit, not only do you feel stronger and healthier, but you acquire soundness of mind as well. When continually practicing physical moves which require having the stamina, and discipline to exercise, you'll develop the qualities that produce self-poise and assuredness. It's also a sure bet that men and women will meet when playing some sort of coed sport.

I can't tell you how many men I've heard complain that, while some women are active, many don't participate in sports, which disappoints them, because this is an area of activity men like to share.

Some women have been taught it's unladylike to sweat. Others have become accustomed to a life-style of sweat-free living. Still others haven't had an interest in sports, finding them too competitive or, perhaps at one time they were harangued to perform. Whatever the reason, it may be time to make a transition into a new direction, while keeping an open-mind, and seriously contemplate joining such activities.

Maybe we women don't want to look foolish by fumbling the ball, getting dirty, or mussing our hair. I must admit, I don't swim as much as I'd like, because it takes so much time to blow-dry my hair. Now I swim only on weekends and participate in such activities as walking or golf during the week.

For a few men and women, one of the reasons sports don't rate on the top of their must-do lists is because they aren't happy with their bodies so don't go out. This creates a double bind because activity makes a person feel better. Remaining indoors and staying inactive only perpetuates the problem and one stays trapped. Accepting who we are—inside and out—gives us the freedom to do whatever we wish. That includes joining a sports team or class.

If you haven't experienced a physical life-style for awhile, begin an activity such as bowling or country-western dancing; neither are overly strenuous. Once you gain confidence, advance to something more challenging, as tennis or scuba diving. My mother is sixty-nine and takes tap-dancing classes, if she can do it, you can too.

Exercising is beneficial in capturing feelings of pleasure because, as you continually move, your brain begins to release endorphins, a hormonal secretion similar to that of morphine, which gives one a feeling of well-being. Playing outdoors also helps to relinquish "WASTE"—an acronym that stands for Worry, Anger, Stress, Troubles, and Ego-

tism. I use it to remind myself why I need to move my body—
to rid myself of WASTE!

Joining others in a physical activity for the first time usually turns out to be less frightening than you'd expect. The thought of doing something new is usually more threatening than the experience itself.

As you recognize your potential and gain confidence in your mental discipline and body's physical abilities, you may come to enjoy sporting endeavors. In so doing, you'll increase the probability of attracting a partner.

If for some reason you can't participate in athletic ventures, knowing your limitations and working within your abilities is commendable. There are many other forms of social activities in which to participate. Work within your scope of capability.

Prescription for where to go

Teams and/or classes are wonderful outlets to generate the exercise we all need to stay sound. Doing something healthy and exhilarating, while meeting people at the same time is a plus. Challenge your abilities by participating in a sport you've always been curious about, or interested in trying.

Here's a list of coed sports ad places to locate them:

- Archery: an archery club; sports club; an archery association
- Backpacking: a sports club; singles club; outdoors club; a hiking organization
- Badminton: a private club; sports club; singles group; a badminton organization

- Baseball: a sponsor; an organization or association; friends; a singles group; a community or recreation center
- Biking: a biking organization; a biking club; a sport and athletic club; a singles association
- Boating: (sail, paddle, or powerboats) boating clubs; boating associations; singles organizations
- Bowling: a bowling facility; a sports organization; a league through your work; a singles club; bowling associations
- Canoeing: a club; a rental facility; a sporting organization
- Cross-country skiing: a rental facility; a club; a sports association; a singles organization
- Dancing: a nightclub; a private dance school or facility; a singles club; a college class; an adult school class
- Fishing: a fishing club or organization
- Golf: a public course; community college or adult school; through a singles or sports organization; a private golf club
- Hiking: a sports or singles organization, or a hiking association or club
- Horseback riding: private stables; through a singles or sports organization; a horseback riding club
- Hot air ballooning: the business itself; a singles or sports club; a ballooning association
- Ice-skating: a facility; a sports organization; a singles club; an ice-skating association
- Jogging: a group; a jogging organization or club; a class through adult school or college; a singles association or sports club; five K run/walk events

- Kayaking: a sports or singles club; a rental facility; a kayaking organization
- Kick boxing: a private facility; a singles group; an athletic club
- Martial arts: the facility itself; a college class; an adult school class
- Mountaineering: a sports organization; a singles association; a mountaineering club
- Roller-skating or roller-blading: a rental facility; a sports club; a singles organization; a roller skating/blading association
- Rowing: a rowing club at a facility; an athletic association; a singles club; a rowing organization
- Sailing: a sailing association; a yacht club; a singles organization; a sports club; an adult school class; a private school
- Scuba diving: a scuba diving club; through the rental equipment facility; a singles or sporting organization; a class
- Sky diving: the business itself; a group; a skydiving association
- Snow skiing: a ski club; a class; a ski association; a rental facility; a singles or sports organization
- Spinning: a gym, or a private facility
- Swimming: an organization; a sports club; community college; recreation center; a swimming facility
- Tennis: a tennis club; a country club; an apartment or community center; a recreation center; the park; through a singles or sports organization; adult school or community college; a resort
- Volleyball: the beach; a gymnasium; community college;

recreation center; a singles or sporting organization or association
- Walking: a group; a singles or sports organization; a walking or race walking club; a class; a walking association; five K walk/run events

Cures for what to do

Participate in coed groups. Be positive, have fun, and make friends. Ask yourself this question, "Would you want to meet you?" Give it some thought. What kind of person do you see? Think about what you like and dislike about yourself. Is there anything you have the power to change? If so, what would it be, and how would you go about it? Take a moment to write down some answers, or close your eyes and visualize yourself in a specific situation. How are you behaving?

While commencing this exercise I visualized myself at a dance—the way I usually feel at a dance—anxious and tense. I pictured myself standing at the periphery of the dance floor, my arms folded across my chest in a serious manner. I then realized this is my normal stance at one of these functions and was as uninviting and closed off as anyone could look. I certainly wouldn't want to approach me. Since then, I've made a consorted effort to position myself in a more open fashion.

For Women

Join teams with a large ratio of men, such as: bicycling, boating, mountaineering, backpacking, or baseball. Unfortunately, many men join sports that are quite physically demanding. Sometimes it's best to take a beginner's class before partaking in the activities where most men go.

<u>For Men</u>

Connect with teams that have the largest ratio of women, such as: bowling, tennis, golf, dancing, or volleyball—sports that aren't intensely physically demanding.

First-aid procedures for breaking the ice

Get involved. Be complimentary when someone performs well for the team. Say, "Good catch," or "Nice going." Prompt a somewhat humorous remark, "Great hit, another Mark McGuire!" Support the person who wasn't able to perform perfectly by saying "Nice try, you'll get it the next time." Ask participants how long they've been practicing and where they go to purchase equipment.

Having shared experiences with others are what forms bonds and establishes camaraderie. Team efforts substantiate friendships promptly and, in no time, you'll most likely be invited to other social functions through these friendships.

Remedies and tips

Sports are activities you may join alone. There's no need to wait around for a friend to go with you, because you'll be amongst others aspiring to do the same thing.

Investing in your emotional well-being, breathing fresh

air, and moving your body is wholesome and keeps the body, mind, and spirit in top health.

It's also the attitude, not the performance that can make any venture worthwhile. Enjoying the game and not allowing your internal critical voice to pressure you into playing perfectly or berating yourself when you make a mistake is uppermost.

By doing the things that might seem difficult at first, and sticking with it, you may come to realize you're truly living your life, not thinking about living your life. Taking that extra effort is what increases self-esteem and brings about a sense of accomplishment.

More remedies and tips

A side note: When you begin dating, being honest from the start is imperative. People don't want to be deceived or misled into believing there's a potential for marriage, or a long-term relationship, if there isn't one. Believing what someone says is a clue as to how involved you ought to become. Occasionally a person will change his or her stance on marriage and/or commitment, but if that person isn't ready, there's not much you can do about it, so the honesty should be appreciated.

Case studies

Some time ago, a friend named Ruth—a petite, exotic, Latin American brunette—and I, met a couple of great guys. Bound for the beach, we went off to acquire a tan. To our surprise, two good-looking men approached us and asked if we'd join them in a volleyball game. Glancing quizzically at each other, we shrugged our shoulders and simultaneously said, "Why not?"

Their names were Tom and Bob. Tom was spoken for; Bob wasn't—good news for me, because I was attracted to Bob. Besides, Ruth was in the process of a divorce at the time and wasn't ready for another relationship.

Bob and I played on one team, and Ruth and Tom on the other. The four of us enjoyed ourselves so much, that we scheduled ongoing weekly games.

The one I liked, Bob, was a computer programmer and an excellent athlete. I happened to enjoy athletics as well and became quite good at the game. Through practice, Bob and I proved to be an unbeatable pair. The four of us played volleyball all summer, and although Tom and Ruth won very few games, they were great sports! Bob and I dated for quite awhile. Although the relationship grew to nothing past friendship, we enjoyed spending quality time together. In retrospect, those were some of the best times of my life, being outdoors; physically fit; gathering with good friends; in a wholesome environment.

***

Mike was a construction worker, and because his occupation was so stereotypical of picking up babes using the infamous "wolf whistle" approach; he knew he needed to find a way to meet women in his spare-time, while doing things he enjoyed. He certainly wouldn't meet women on the job.

At a party one evening, he came up with the idea to form a co-ed baseball team and invited the lot of them to try out the very next day. Mike's venture materialized, and a few weeks later he began seeing one of the gals on the team named Joan.

They dated throughout the season and got to know one another well enough to realize that, although they had physical chemistry and baseball in common, in the end, their values were dissimilar.

I use this as an example for three reasons: the first, as a presentation of how Mike created his own sports team. Second, as an example of why we date—to acquire enough information about one another to determine if we have qualities and values that would endure a meaningful relationship and withstand the test of time. And third, that the reality of dating is that we must be willing to meet many people, not everyone will be a match.

Research and development for finding sports teams and/or classes

Bookstores and Libraries

Bookstores—check the sports, entertainment, and recreation sections of the bookstore. Also check the magazine section for sports and hobbies.

Libraries—look in the reference section of the library for The Gale Encyclopedia of Associations—a comprehensive directory for any type of association, including sports. The encyclopedia provides phone numbers and addresses for the sport of your liking.

The Internet

Contact http://www.sport-hq.com/, America's Sports H.Q.: "the Web's sports directory." They list everything from lawn bowling to skydiving. Highlight the sport of your interest, and then find a league or association in your area and click on the schedule of events. They provide addresses, phone numbers, or e-mail addresses for contact.

Newspapers

The entertainment, life-style, sports, or regional sections of your newspaper have information on sports and activities. Check those sections, especially on Thursdays or Fridays, when most newspapers have the greatest amount of information regarding activities for the upcoming weekend. Check the newspaper every week for new and fun things to do.

Examine the city's free, weekly papers, which list local events.

Utilize the Phone Book

The White Pages list the names of businesses. Check sporting goods dealers and/or equipment stores, sports clubs, or the YMCA, for classes.

The Yellow Pages carry listings of schools, both public and private; call for a catalog of classes. Check the specific sport by name, such as swimming or dancing, to see what's listed.

The government section is usually located in the front of the phone directory and lists state, county, and city schools, in addition to universities. Call the school for a catalog. While in the government section, look under the name of your city or county to find the nearest recreation center and call for a brochure. Also try checking under the heading of public facilities and resources departments.

Sporting Goods and Equipment Retailers

These stores sometimes carry information at the front counter or on a bulletin board for upcoming classes and events. They may also have catalogs or directories for sporting activities. Call to ask the clerk or store manager what type of information they can provide.

Here are a few national associations or organizations:

The International Sail and Power Association
This is an association for boating enthusiasts.
(800) 987-5494.

The American Alpine Club
For people interested in mountaineering.
(303) 384-0110.

The American Hiking Society
P.O. Box 20160
Washington, DC 20041
(202) 565-6704
This group promotes hiking and recommends foot trails in America. The Web site address is www.orca.org/AHS/. Call for publications, such as newsletters or magazines.

The National Archery Association of the U.S.
1 Olympic Plaza
Colorado Springs, CO 80909-5778
(719) 578-4576 Phone
(719) 632-4733 Fax
Serves individuals or clubs interested in target archery. Call for their newsletter or for information on competitions and/or meetings.

The U.S. Badminton Association
1 Olympic Plaza
Colorado Springs, CO 80909-5778
(719) 578-4808
Assists in helping to develop clubs or associations interested in badminton. Call for a newsletter or magazine.

The American Canoe Association
Springfield, Virginia
(703) 451-0141
This association is dedicated to the sport of canoeing and kayaking. Call for a newsletter or magazine.

The League of American Bicyclists
Baltimore, Maryland
(800) 288-BIKE
Promotes bicycling for both recreational and functional transportation uses. Call for a newsletter or magazine.

American Trails in Washington DC
(202) 797-5418

Provides information on trails, conferences, and activities. Call for a newsletter or information.

Start Your Own

Begin a team, club, or league of your own. Many employers are supportive of leagues or teams representing their companies. You could also run an ad in the paper for a start-up team. Or, through word-of-mouth, get friends together and have them invite their friends. Convince a recreational facility to assist you in starting a team or class.

Get something going through your apartment or condominium complex or neighborhood by posting a bulletin, or arrange for your chosen sport's association to help you advertise.

Miscellaneous

Check bulletin boards for flyers in grocery stores, laundromats, libraries, or community centers for posted activities.

Get Competitive ... Games and Indoor Recreation

Therapeutic attitudes

What good is meeting people if you have nothing to say?

Whether playing pool, bowling, or checkers, it's difficult to meet others if you don't know what to say. By reading the newspaper, you'll gain information for conversation beginnings. Skimming each section daily and reading a few articles; provides you with topics for discussion. Even by watching TV news or listening to talk-radio, you're able to stay on top of current events. You'll feel fairly confident you can carry on a dialogue without feeling uninformed. You can participate in conversations and even bring up topics because you'll know what to say.

The following is one of my favorite examples of an impressive social outcome, brought about after reviewing the newspaper. For some reason, I decided to read an article on cattle. I found it interesting at the time and thought no more of it. Two days later, I met a rancher at a putting course.

I rarely meet ranchers, mind you, but that day I did, and to my amazement, we were able to have an interesting conversation concerning livestock. Now and then I see him at the golf center. We have an affinity toward one another because of our initial conversation.

No great level of expertise is necessary, but having a little knowledge on many subjects, promotes a more companionable presence and makes it possible to converse with people from many walks of life: from the "rich and famous, to the poor and unknown."

Prescription for where to go

Listed below are ideas for games and indoor recreation and where to find them:

- Backgammon: a privately owned facility such as a night-club; a community organization or recreation center
- Badminton: a privately owned facility such as a country club; a singles group; a badminton organization or club
- Billiards or Pool: a privately owned facility; a singles club; a billiard/pool organization
- Bingo: a club; a singles group; an organization
- Bowling: a privately owned facility; an organization; a singles group
- Card games: (such as bridge, gin, poker, or blackjack) at clubs; casinos; organizations
- Checkers: a club; a singles group; recreation center; an organization
- Chess: a club; a singles group; a recreation center; an association

- Darts: a singles organization; a recreation center; pubs and/or sports bars
- Foosball: a privately owned facility such as; a bar or pub; an arcade
- Handball: a recreation center; a singles group; a park; an association
- Miniature Golf: a privately owned facility, a singles group; an organization
- Ping-Pong: (also referred to as table tennis or paddle tennis) a recreation center; a resort; a country club; a group
- Putting Courses: a privately owned facility (This is a fairly new public activity so availability may be limited)
- Racquetball: a privately owned facility; a club; an organization
- Shuffleboard: a recreation center; a group; an organization
- Video games: privately owned arcades or nightclubs

Cures for what to do

Since the nature of games is interactive, it's an easy way to meet people. If you live in an area where the weather restricts outdoor activity, rather than staying home-bound, waiting for the weather to change . . . go out.

If you live near a gaming facility, make it your home away from home. Get to know the staff and the customers. By making friends with people of all ages, you'll expand your network of acquaintances. Don't restrict yourself to fraternizing with only the opposite sex. Some of my girlfriends have met their mates through other women, and some men have met their wives through their male friends.

You need only to show up, and eventually you'll meet people. Ask someone to lunch or to go out for coffee, or ask for a phone number. If you haven't dated in awhile and are intimidated by your lack of practice; go out on dates with people who are nonthreatening; someone you'd consider a friend as opposed to someone with whom you're sexually attracted.

For Men

The following is an honest and straightforward way to approach a woman for a date. "Excuse me, but there's something about you that intrigues me, if you're free, I'd like to take you to out for coffee sometime." Most women are flattered and aren't insulted or scared by this approach.

Remedies and tips

People have a tendency to look for someone who's perfect, and I'm no exception. One of my past failings is that I wanted someone to fit the entire bill; desirous of every quality I wanted in a man. But the reality was, when I found someone with ambition—he was lacking in the romance department; when I found someone with passion—he was self-deceptive; when I came across a guy who was generous—he was critical. The list is as long as there are men or women.

By coming to terms with the fact that no man or woman will be the perfect prince or princess, we're able to choose a companion with whom we can tolerate certain shortcomings. Knowing which faults you're able to withstand is a vital part of choosing a partner. For instance, you may be able to accept a person who's a bit reserved or subdued, but unable to endure someone with a lack of ambition. When you know this, you don't have to waste time with people you'll not respect in the long run. Having respect for one another is a basic necessity for a long-term relationship.

If we want to love and be loved, we must be willing to accept another's flaws as a part of the package. In addition, in order to find someone who knows how to love, be someone who loves. In order for someone to stick with you through thick and thin, be someone who sticks with him or her through thick and thin.

If you're feeling sad or angry; unable to change your thoughts or feelings toward loving yourself and/or others, there are many resources for help. Overcoming obstacles in one's psyche, in order to have a quality love life, is often complex without help. Try counseling, or perhaps a twelve-step program geared toward your particular difficulty, or spiritual guidance through a specific religious affiliation.

Resource

Read *How to Stop Looking for Somebody Perfect and Find Somebody to Love* by Judith Sills Ph.D. It will help you do just that, or her latest book for women, a similar yet updated variation of that booked called, *Biting the Apple*. All of Judith Sill's books are commendable and helpful in the relationship arena.

First-aid procedures for breaking the ice

Some common conversational openers while playing games:

"You seem pretty good at this. Have you been playing long?"

"I'd like to know more about this. Would you mind showing me how?"

"I'm having a few people over for dinner and to play cards. Since you enjoy games, you're invited to join us if you'd like."

"I've heard there's a new game room in town, called The New Game Room in Town, have you heard of it?"

"Do you know of other billiard rooms in the area? My brother will be in town next week and I'd like to show him a few spots."

"I'll bet a dollar I can beat you at the next game."

"I'm new to the area, do you know of other places to play?"

Case studies

Vickie, a college student at UCI, was procrastinating— avoiding her books one night— when she remembered the billiard room across the street.

Her parents owned a pool table so she was quite familiar with the game. Vickie figured hitting a few balls would clear her mind and then, maybe she could get back to her studies, refreshed.

While setting up and breaking the rack of balls, Vickie could feel someone looking her way. It turned out to be a very handsome guy named Sean—also a student. She felt attracted to him immediately. He asked if he could play a game with her, she said, "Sure."

They played and talked throughout the evening. He asked for her phone number, and arranged to see her again soon. Within the week, he took her to dinner. He brought flowers, candy, gifts —never empty-handed. She found him irresistible. Sean and Vickie graduated and were married soon after. Now they have three adorable children.

* * *

Here's an example of the importance of being friendly with everyone you meet: a former co-worker, Barbara—a petite, brunette nurse, wanted to go out with Pete, a policeman we both knew. However, because she was shy, when he asked her out, she said, "Only if you get Gail a date and we double." So Pete agreed.

The day came for the double date, when Barbara and I drove to the designated restaurant. It was arranged that we would go to dinner then play arcade games afterward. Pete invited his friend Phillip. He and Phillip stood in the lobby waiting for us. Pete had neglected to tell Barbara the only single guy he knew was twenty-one. Nor had he told Phillip that his blind date was thirty-eight—an underhanded ploy—even though technically Pete kept his end of the bargain.

So Phillip and I made the best of it. We were friendly, talkative, and managed to get through the evening, making a satisfying time of it. Since we did the best we could in that circumstance, Phillip and I agreed, we were good sports.

51

Before the evening ended, Phillip said he'd like to introduce me to a co-worker of his: a single, forty-three year old, named Ed. He gave Ed my number and we dated for awhile. I told Phillip I would reciprocate when I could, but he responded, "I'm in my twenties, did you have any trouble meeting people when you were in your twenties?"

The situation was an example of using the golden rule. From it, I'd gained not only a dating situation, but a new friend as well.

Research and development for finding indoor recreation and games

The Internet

For games, type: www.sport-hq.com/America's Sports H.Q.: "the Web's sports directory." Games are listed on this site. Or, type in the name of the game you want, such as "chess" and surf the Web.

The Newspaper

The calendar section of the newspaper carries different events each week. The sports section sometimes lists of pubs and/or taverns that may cater to games. The entertainment section highlights upcoming events and usually provides a review.

Utilizing the Phone Directory

The Yellow Pages list both places to go, and the game itself. Check binary listings. Look under taverns, racquet clubs, arcades, sports bars, nightclubs, amusement, or recreation centers. Or, look up billiards, video games, darts, and the like.

The government section in the front of the telephone book lists the name of your city and surrounding cities. From there check for recreation centers or other public facilities that hold games.

The White Pages list businesses by name, alphabetically of course. Sometimes businesses will list only in the white pages to save on cost.

Get Enthusiastic … Indoor and outdoor activities

Therapeutic Attitudes

When you're in public, keep your antenna up

For Women

When in a crowd, pay attention to how many men are looking your way. Most men would agree that they intuit a woman who feels feminine and confident from her mannerisms. You might be surprised to discover how many opportunities there are for flirting when you keep your eyes open. Of course you won't know this if you're looking down or staring straight ahead. Keep your head up, your mind alert, "your antenna up," and smile.

For Men

Keep your focus on women who smile at you. While outdoors, in your leisure time, take notice if someone is checking you out. Some of us tend to be shy at times—myself included—so don't flirt in public often; but when in a daring or confident mood, try it. Remember that you don't have to be at an "event" to get a date. If you notice a woman smiling at you say, "Hi." Or ask, "Are you going my way?" or, "May I walk you to your destination?"

Women sense when a man is feeling confident and in charge of his life, and these are the men who ask women out wherever they go.

My friend Eileen gets stopped most everywhere, once even, in a discount-clothing store. I've literally been stopped and asked for a date while in the middle of a crosswalk, while strolling along the beach, walking my dog, driving in the car, and in front of a video store. I must admit, the times I'm acknowledged are when I feel physically fit and happy. Usually in the spring and summertime, when most people feel good to be outdoors again and come alive. Most women admire men who have the courage to approach them for a date.

Some case histories

The following are some example of meeting while outdoors:

Pumping gas

Norma, a purchasing agent for the hospital, met her husband, Ted, at the gas pump. She had trouble unscrewing the gas cap and asked the man at the next stall for help. He assisted in removing the cap for her; then invited her to lunch. She agreed to meet him a few hours later. During the meal, they discovered they had mutual friends and much in common. Such a coincidence amazed them both and they dated from that moment on, until their wedding day.

Taking out the trash

Valerie, an attractive esthetician, met her husband while hauling her trash cans out to the roadside curb. Milton, a tall, blonde, computer software salesman, lived two doors down and was outdoors when he spotted Valerie doing her chores. He thought she was cute, walked over to her, and began a conversation. After confirming her eligibility, he invited her to a neighborhood barbecue at his house—an undertaking he hadn't done before or since.

Valerie didn't think Milton was her type, but she kept going out with him because there was no reason to break it off. Much to her surprise, after three months, she found he was one of the most attentive, good-hearted men she'd ever met. Appreciating these qualities in him, her admiration and respect for him grew, until she understood he was the one she truly loved and, in the end, married.

In the apartment complex

Jennifer, a nurse and diabetes educator, met her husband in her apartment complex. Jeff noticed her as she moved in and asked if he could help with the heavy boxes. She was happy to have the extra assistance. For the next few weeks he stopped to chat. Shortly after, he offered to take her to a new local restaurant, and she agreed to go. She thought him charming, and appreciated his determination in pursuing her. Last year they were married. This year they had a bouncing baby boy.

<u>On the boat to Catalina Island</u>

Virginia met Charlie on the boat to Catalina, on which she traveled often to visit her aunt. She and Charlie chatted on one of her trips over from San Pedro. Virginia enjoyed his company, but when on land, they said their good-byes.

She dismissed the encounter as yet another pleasant trip on the boat and no more. But being the small island that it is, they ran into each other all weekend. Finally Charlie said, "Look we keep bumping into one another, I think someone is trying to tell you that you ought to have dinner with me. Let me take you to The Big Portion Restaurant tonight. We'll probably wind up in the same place anyway." How could she oppose? From that evening on, the dinners never stopped. They're still dating and have plans to be married and move to Hawaii.

Prescription for where to go

Indoor and outdoor activities that may be either organized or informal:

- Amusement Parks: theme parks, water parks, and the like
- Beaches: public, private, county, or state
- Bookstores: independent or chain stores
- Carnivals: community, county, fund-raising
- Concerts: rock and roll, classical, reggae, jazz, and so forth
- Fairs: county, cultural, agricultural, or community

- Festivals: cultural, dance, agricultural, art, music, food and wine tasting, community
- Galleries: art, history, or science
- Lakes: man made or natural
- Laundromats: in or around town
- Mountains: high or low-lying
- Museums: art, science, history, or specialty
- Parks: local, county, or state
- Pools: public, private, or community
- Rivers: large or small
- Shopping: in malls, tourist shops, specialty shops, or gift stores
- Sightseeing: by bus, foot, or tour guide
- Trails: long or short
- Traveling: on busses, airplanes, boats, or other transportation modes
- Zoos: city or county

First-aid procedures for breaking the ice

If you're going to be relaxing outdoors by the pool or at the beach, bring a book with an unusual title as—*Eat the Rich*. Notice if others are reading—if so, comment on their books.

Bring a flamboyant blanket or unusual towel, or remark on someone else's. For example: if a person has a towel with a picture of Popeye the cartoon character on it, you could say, "Is that a self portrait?" or "Got any spinach?" or "You are what you are, right?"

Pets are wonderful icebreakers. Take your dog with you

to a lake or stream. If you don't have a dog, borrow a neighbor's dog and stroll with it. Comment on other people's pets. Inquire as to the breed of dog, or its name. Pigs are adorable. Anyone I know would approach someone with a pet pig, or any cute animal for that matter. Bring a bird, a snake, or a rabbit with you. Welcome the comments as they come streaming in.

While browsing through a pet store recently, I noted a leash made specifically for a hamster. Who wouldn't comment seeing a hamster on a leash?

By the way, I hope these creatures are used to meet others, only because you enjoy animals and have them as pets anyway, not solely for attracting men or women; otherwise, they aren't good ideas.

Remedies and tips

If you're open to talking and smiling to people wherever you go, you may be surprised as to the outcome. The following is an example of how smiling helped Amy through a difficult evening. Amy, being somewhat serious by nature and not a "smiler," was having a miserable time at a dance. Dances always made her feel uncomfortable. The too loud music, coupled with the rowdy people, packed in the joint like sardines, added to Amy's discomfort. Since she knew she wouldn't be there for more than an hour, she pretended to be enjoying herself by smiling. Suddenly, others were smiling back—and even saying hello! To her amazement, the dance unexpectedly, turned tolerable. She began to feel happy in spite of herself!

It was then, she realized, smiling creates an appearance of gaiety and amiability—a sign of approachability. If it works in crowded, rowdy nightclubs, imagine what it could do in an environment where she felt comfortable. Amy learned a valuable lesson from what began as a seemingly deplorable event.

Resource

The New Personality Self-Portrait by John Oldham, M.D., is an excellent book about understanding yourself and others. It explains how personalities are inherited traits, being largely genetic. His text also accounts for why children, all raised in the same family, may have completely different temperaments. In addition, it informs you of love matches and careers, suited to your personality type. It's a favorite of mine for understanding human behavior and constitutional makeup.

Case study

Hava, a nurse at work, met her husband while walking her dog. His dog tried to attack hers. He pulled his dog away, apologized, and asked to take her out sometime, promising to leave his dog at home. He took her phone number and called two days later for a dinner date. They had an exceptional time together and commenced dating twice a week for months. After the sixth month, he asked her to marry him. She said yes, but only if he'd agree to a long engagement. He did, and they married a year and a half later.

Research and development for finding indoor and outdoor activities

Find an outdoor or indoor activity based on what you like to do. However, just by venturing out-of-doors, you might meet someone.

Bookstores

Travel books are often excellent sources for ideas about outdoor endeavors. Also try the Zagat's guides. They're full of reliable places to go for dining, hotels, or sightseeing.

Check the many magazines that are devoted to travel, and entertainment. Metropolitan magazines also feature activities.

Look up some book titles on the Internet at the following addresses: http://www.amazon.com, www.bo·ders.com, or www.barnesandnoble.com.

Try bookstores such as, Walden Books. Book-A-Million, or any independent bookstore.

Also check catalogs that carry books.

Hotels

A hotel concierge has information regarding indoor and outdoor activities. They carry pamphlets, catalogs, and bulletins for things to do—both in town, and regionally.

The Internet

Search the Internet for the activity of your interest by typing in the name of the activity, such as museums, art galleries, or zoos, plus the name of your city, surrounding cities, or county. When you set the subject and city in quotation marks, the search becomes more specific.

Checking the Newspapers

Check the entertainment, travel, or life-style sections of the newspaper at least once a week for activities.

Utilizing the phone book

The Yellow Pages list subject matter. Check topics such as amusement or entertainment.

The White Pages list places of business by title. Perhaps you have a favorite travel agent. Call your agent for ideas concerning things to do and places to go, such as concerts or flea markets.

The government section lists the name of your city, or surrounding cities, where you may check the parks and recreation departments. Call your local city hall, they may be able to direct you to a department that lists community events.

* * *

AAA Club has a magazine that publicizes events such as fairs and festivals. Call the local regional office in your area. The nationwide number is (800) 680-AAA4. Travel agents are available within this organization, who have access to information on almost anything you'd like to do in this arena.

Some phone numbers and/or addresses for things to do:

Vanderbilt Museum
Centerport, NY
(516) 854-5555

The International Association of Fairs and Expositions
3043 E. Cairo Street #985
Springfield, MO 65802-6204
(417) 862-5771
Provides a newsletter on fairs and expositions nationwide.

The San Diego Zoo
2920 Zoo Dr.
San Diego, CA 92103
(619) 234-3153

Maui Ocean Center
192 Maalaea Road
Wailuku, Maui
HI 96793 USA
(808) 270-7000

Oakhill Center for Rare and Endangered Species
19800 E. Coffee Creek Road
Luther, OK 73054
(405) 277-9354

Woodruff Arts Center
1280 Peachtree St. NE
Atlanta, GA 30309
(404) 733-HIGH

Attending mind-broadening functions is a plus, whether you meet the man or woman of your dreams, or not. My girlfriend Theresa and I used to promise to do one cultural activity per month in order to keep informed and refined. This way we continually increased our level of education, inspiration, and creativity.

I've not been to all locations and am unable to vouch for them personally, but the list may prompt your imagination for something else to do.

Get Buzzed … Coffeeshops

Therapeutic attitudes

Contagious hot spots

Coffeehouses are designed for people to hang out, which spreads sociability like a contagion. The soda fountain of the fifties has now become the coffeehouse of the new millennium. Many people spend time there to be amongst people while studying or doing paperwork. Some write letters, create poetry, or draw. Others play checkers, card games, and the like.

As you hang out in a coffeehouse or anywhere for that matter, take note of others' stances or body language. It's the first thing one notices of another. The way a person sits, stands, or moves can have significant meaning. For instance: when closed off to meeting others, some people literally encase their bodies by crossing their arms and legs. This signals others to keep their distance, implying there's no interest in being approached. Avoiding eye contact is another way of demonstrating disinterest or perhaps shyness.

Conversely, allowing your arms to hang at your side, keeping your body unrestricted; presents a more receptive persona. This will draw people toward you, lending itself to a positive epidemic of "receiving attention."

Take it a step further and think creative, marvelous thoughts about people. According to many intercommunication books, only ten percent of interaction is through language. The other ninety- percent is by way of voice-intonation, body-gestures, and vibrations or energy. Because people have the ability to sense an amicable presence, thinking caring thoughts will remarkably draw people to you.

Open body posturing creates an appearance of approachability. Who knows, after practicing the discipline of virtuous thinking long enough, you may even acquire some new facial expressions or mannerisms.

To meet others, spend some time in a coffeehouse alone. Sit in a chair and stay there for a predetermined duration. Eventually someone will initiate a conversation or respond to yours. I tried it and, after a while, wound up talking to the owner of the coffeehouse. He taught me the process of how he roasts coffee beans each morning. I learned where his shipments originate; in what condition they arrive; his acceptance or rejection of particular beans; and so on.

I found it interesting to hear of another's livelihood and discover things I'd not have known otherwise. You may be surprised at the results when you converse with those who cross your path and find that interacting with others isn't really difficult.

Here's a special and useful saying by Frank Outlaw, reminding us of the reason we need to think for right purpose:

Watch your thoughts; they become your words.
Watch your words; they become your actions.

Watch your actions; they become your habits.
Watch your habits; they become your character.
Watch your character; it becomes your destiny.

What a wonderful reminder to help us to stay on track with principled thinking and useful deeds. There's a great deal of temptation to be lazy, unrestrained, or lax in our self-governing, which originates with our thoughts. We're all presented with opportunities to be disrespectful, think negatively of one another, or become judgmental. By considering and practicing the above principles, we'll attract more love into our lives—even in a coffeehouse.

In Emmet Fox's book, *Sermon on the Mount*, he states "If you want a congenial companion and be loved; you must first think thoughts of love and goodwill."

Prescription for where to go

Coffeehouses have sprung up nationwide; however, if you don't have a coffeehouse in your vicinity, a coffee shop or restaurant will do.

Cures for what to do

By stopping in at a coffeehouse routinely you'll meet occasional and regular customers and get to know the employees. These people may be good contacts for meeting others, or some you may want to date.

While sitting in a coffeehouse, bring magazines to thumb through, take a book with an unusual title, such as *Insomnia*, or one containing gorgeous pictures. In this context, these may be seen as props, but, in actuality, they're activities you'd normally do, so why not bring them to a coffeehouse where opportunities could open up to meet somebody?

Don't pass up a chance to comment on someone else's paraphernalia. For instance, if someone's reading the book entitled, *The Seven Habits of Highly Effective People*. Ask which of the habits they think are most effective. Maybe they're reading *911-Urgent Dating Solutions*. You might ask which of the solutions work best . . . and if they're busy tonight.

Many coffeehouses have open-mike night, which means: persons interested in performing are welcome to sign up as a part of that evening's featured entertainment. This usually includes any or all or the following: music, singing, poetry reading, or comedy.

Bring your laptop or desk chores with you to a coffeehouse instead of doing them at home alone. If you don't meet anyone, there certainly isn't anything lost—you've accomplished your laptop endeavor or home chore anyhow.

Coffeehouses have their own unique personalities that attract particular clientele. Business districts or cultural areas of town are likely choices when seeking to meet eligible single people. Coffeehouses near theatres, shopping malls, or tourist areas are also good choices.

Time of day is another consideration. Early morning draws working people. Mid-morning may be when students, evening shift workers, or self-employed individuals show up. Noon would be break-time for the employed. Evenings are when most places offer entertainment, and perhaps more singles unite.

Experiment with locations and times to determine which

is right for you. Once you've found a suitable spot, stick with it, become a familiar face. When you're accustomed with your surroundings, your body moves more naturally, creating a relaxed energy exchange and consequently better results for meeting others.

First-aid procedures for breaking the ice

Ask simple questions of someone:
- "Is that a cafe mocha or a latte?"
- "How's that iced coffee? I've been wondering about ordering it."
- "Have you tried their muffins? They look good."
- "Would you happen to know if they have musical entertainment here?"
- "I see you're reading *Looking for Mr. Goodbook*, I've heard it's excellent. What do you think?"
- "My playing partner didn't show up, would you like to play a game with me?"

Children ask questions and make friends this easily. We adults become much too serious, and far too busy. We ought to take lessons from children by simply speaking up and interact with others, while enjoying uncomplicated moments in time, as they do.

Remedies and tips

If you're in a coffeehouse watching a performer, be it a poet or a singer—compliment that person on some aspect of his or her performance after the show. It may seem that an entertainer has an easy time of expressing him or herself in front of others, but it isn't always easy. Everyone feels the fear of rejection, failure, or gut-wrenching stage fright at times. You never know the impact you may have on another when you compliment someone on a job well done.

Looking beyond yourself and focusing on what you can give to others is really what life is all about. Not only does it make someone else feel good, but it causes you to feel even better! And, who knows—you could form a friendship.

I met a wonderful saxophone player by complementing him after a show. He was a marvelous musician and entertainer. He interacted with the crowd by stepping off stage, playing directly to a few audience members, while at the same time, forming funny gestures with his face and body. People were thoroughly entertained and involved in his music and antics. His display of talent and casual, friendly manner, inspired me.

What a gift he had, and how gallantly he expressed his ability. I thanked him afterwards, revealing my gratitude for such a wonderful performance. Later that summer I saw him at a few other events. He remembered me because of the sincere appreciation and respect I'd shown him previously.

One of my most cherished memories is when he invited me to accompany him as the vocalist for a few jazz tunes when he played at an outdoor cafe. If I hadn't taken the time to praise that wonderful musician, I'd have missed out on one of my most treasured moments in time. A distinct example of what happens when we give to others. Extraordinary things can happen when we show up to places other than our living rooms.

Some people may not think of my experience as an awesome situation, but I've come to learn that's it's the little things in life— the simple, perhaps unspectacular moments we live, that renew our passion for life. When we feel full of appreciation, others recognize it and we're attractive.

Resource

Read *1001 Ways to Be Romantic*, by Gregory J.P. Godek, it moves one to treat special people romantically. His ideas can be used for motivation to continue dating, so that when a loved one is met, one knows the gestures to practice with him or her.

Case Studies

I met a woman named Carol, while writing this book. She was a hotel's concierge. She inquired as to what sort of book I was writing. When I told her it was a book about where to go and what to do to get a date and maybe fall in love; she said she met somebody special at a coffeehouse and told me her story.

Carol and her friend Dorothy were sitting outdoors, listening to live music one evening at a coffeehouse, when a friend of Dorothy's, named Monty strolled by.

He'd stepped in to purchase a cup of coffee. A large one, for he was an engineer and wanted to stay awake long enough to finish a project at work.

He seemed, however, open to socializing, because when Dorothy called out his name, he smiled and sat down to chat with them awhile. Carol was excited and astounded to discover that she and Monty had many of the same interests. He liked to hike, had a passion for gourmet cooking, and held season tickets for plays at the local theatre. By the time he finished his coffee, he asked Carol for her phone number. He took her to the theatre and they've been together ever since.

***

A friend named Keeley, and a waitress at a coffee shop, served coffee and toast to an attorney named Ron, every Monday through Friday, at seven a.m. He told her he and his wife were divorcing, and that he was lonely. He asked Keeley if she had any friends she could introduce him to. Keeley's friend, Pam came to mind. When Keeley phoned her, Pam agreed to have Ron call. He asked her for a date that week. Ron took her out and they dated for months. Although it didn't last, he continued to meet acquaintances and friends through Keeley. Ron found a way of making connections by becoming friends with the waitress at the coffee shop.

***

I used to stop in at a coffeehouse where a group of comedian friends performed on open-mike night. Mary, Who's a hilarious comedienne and attorney, met her boyfriend Jim, a landscaper and also a comedian, at that coffeehouse.

We practiced our comedy every Wednesday night. Mary and Jim's interest in each other grew as they got to know each other. I haven't been there for a while now, but the last time I talked to Mary, she told me that being with Jim makes her feel like a schoolgirl again. The impassioned sense of being in love for the first time; a glowing sensation and flushing of the skin; an accelerated heart rate; inability to eat or sleep; thinking only of when you'll see your lover again. Anyway, you get the picture.

So, when you want to meet people at a coffeehouse, show up on a routine basis, as Mary and Jim did.

Research and development for finding a coffeehouse

Around Town

Watch for coffeehouses as you're driving around town. Stop to chat with the owner or personnel. Check to see if they have flyers or announcements regarding entertainment. Ask the employees what types of customers frequent the establishment.

Word of Mouth

Quiz your friends and acquaintances. Find out if they know of any popular coffeehouses where single people hang out. Store clerks, cashiers, and waitress also come in contact with many people and may be privy to such things. Ask your barber, hairdresser, manicurist, or anyone else in touch with the public regarding coffeehouses.

Checking the Newspapers

Events such as poetry reading, comedy, or music are sometimes listed under coffeehouses in the Thursday or

Friday entertainment sections of the newspaper.

Check free local publications found in storefronts or newspaper stands, for regional information, which oftentimes list coffeehouses through ads or upcoming event columns.

Utilizing the Phone Book

The Yellow Pages list coffeehouses under the subject heading of coffee or restaurants.

The White Pages list the coffeehouses by name such as, Starbucks or Dietrichs, both of which are nationwide chains.

Treatment Plan Seven

Get Advertised...Personal ads in newspapers or magazines

(Personal ads for dating via the Internet can be found in the chapter entitled Get High-tech.)

Therapeutic attitudes

Dating momentum

Some people may think personal ads are for social misfits, the unconscionable, or the downright desperate—perhaps some are, but the majorities aren't. Ads are merely a vehicle for people who prefer not to be alone, to get a date.

Oddly enough, human beings seem to inherently intuit others who are dating. It appears to be an irony in life that, when you want to date— no one asks you out. When you're already dating, then the phone rings. An easy solution to that problem is to answer ads once week and place ads once a month. By doing this, you'll be dating, and when others sense it, you initiate momentum for, the more you date . . . the more you're asked out on dates.

Many busy professional people don't have extra time to socialize. Ads are a simple way to become acquainted with people who are single. The people who place and respond to personal ads are motivated simply by the desire to meet others.

People have become isolated from one another more than ever as we continue further into the information age. We're housed in solitary units for individual privacy, we each drive separate cars, and some of us aren't even required to show up for work if we can manage our business by telephone, fax, and/or computer.

Even future nursing hopes are aimed toward the possibility of having vital signs and disease symptoms checked via technological devices at home—reducing the need to see a doctor or have a visiting nurse examine you.

I'm sure you're all too aware of automated assistance of some sort, especially on the telephone. The proverbial, "Hello, this is *Indifferent Robotics Inc.*; what's your birth date and phone number? What's your address and the number on your account?" We're no longer addressed first and foremost as human beings. When did the "corporate machine" stop asking for our names?

This is one of the many examples of dehumanization, in our changing world. And so the detachment rolls off into all areas of our lives. We work long hours, have responsibilities and obligations that take up our time, and it's becoming a rarity to find an open interval in which to socialize. Since we're tired, and last month, went to three coffeehouses, two gyms, and a partridge in a pear tree, and met no one we wanted to date, we place ads . . .pure and simple.

It's actually been my experience and pleasure, to encounter some of the most fascinating, intelligent, and talented people I've ever met through personal ads. Some of their professions have been: hospital administrators; business managers; entrepreneurs; land developers; therapists; audiologists; architects; even a rocket scientist! I kid you not. Most of them white-collar professionals, only because that's my preference, however, all types of people use personal ads.

I don't want to mislead you either; there have been some strange, frightened, angry, rude, and sloppy people in the mix. But, by developing the ability to endure the good with the bad; remain in high spirits; and even the value the weird experiences, you gain tolerance—an unforeseen virtue. In addition, one can have the privilege of recounting some of the most hilarious social tales anyone could ever tell.

Finding the right man or woman takes time. You'll be able to more easily accept a disappointing encounter in stride and with grace when you keep that in mind. I've found that for me; when I'm ready to start a new search; it takes about one year, more or less; to find someone to love with whom I have chemistry; who holds my intrigue; and with whom I share interests.

A number of people think personal ads are a horrid way to meet. Yet, those same people will date the new friends if someone else had met them first! The following examples are true stories.

I met Michael, a chiropractor, through the personal ads. As we dated, he told me about his friend Tom, a widower, who was interested in dating. I mentioned Tom to my friend Roberta, who said she'd be delighted to be introduced to Tom. Yet this is the same woman who said, "I wouldn't be caught dead dating someone out of the newspaper ads!" What's the difference?

Another time, I met a man from the personals; a land developer named Richard. We weren't attracted to one another on our initial meeting, but he was a nice guy, so I asked him if he'd like to meet a friend of mine named Cecile. He said he would. When I asked Cecile if I could give him her number, her reply was, "Yes, of course!" She'd have been appalled to say they met through an ad, yet she agreed to meet him for a date, even though that's how I met him!

Sometimes people are fearful of meeting others through advertising. An ad is open to the world. At least in a bar or a gym, one has the illusion of knowing something about the new person, yet there are no guarantees.

Others feel that social introductions should only exist through certain avenues, and that advertising isn't one of them. Some think that if you advertise, you must be pretty hard up, socially graceless, or downright ugly.

You may be missing out on innumerable dates with fine people, by holding on to an outdated attitude. People in their twenties find it fairly easy to get dating partners; because the majority of them are single. Then the thirties crowd has a bit more difficult time; many are already taken. By the time we're in our forties and beyond, if we're single, we've become a minority; and the search for a compatible companion gets tougher.

Dating through the personal ads can be fun. It works. This is a new age; so ignore any stigma attached to it. Don't allow anyone to make you feel bad about dating through the personal ads.

Sometimes people are jealous when they find out how

often you date and how much fun you're having. They'd like to be doing it too. The truth be known; they're too afraid of blind dates; too embarrassed of what someone else might think, including their own thoughts on the subject; or don't want to put forth the effort to meet in this manner.

It's so much easier tolerating singleness when you're dating. Having dates lined up, as well as other activities, creates a feeling of satisfaction. When you're dating, the feeling of being wanted and desirable shows and attracts others.

Prescription for where to go

Check local and regional newspapers and magazines to place and answer ads.

Cures for what to do

I'll review the following facets of advertising:
* Interpreting and screening ads
* Answering an ad
* Placing an ad

Interpreting and screening ads

Upon reading the personal ads, you'll find the advertiser will usually note initial pieces of information: physical appearance; character traits; occupation; hobbies/interests and so forth—in addition to what they're looking for in a partner.

For the sake of space, ads are written in abbreviated style. A sample ad might read:

**Attr. SWF, 5'4" blu/bln. athletic, Skg.
SWM or SHM 33-43 y.o. attr. Prof.
for fun activities and poss. LTR, N/S.**

Translation:

Attr—attractive
SWF—single white female
Blu/bln—blue eyes and blonde hair
Athletic—body build
SWM or SHM—single white male or single Hispanic male
33-43 y.o.—33 to 43 years old and desired age range
Prof—professional
Poss. LTR—possible long-term relationship
N/S—no smoking

Other abbreviations include:
A—Asian
B—African-American or black
C—Christian
D—Divorced
G—Gay
J—Jewish
L—Lesbian
N/D—Non-Drinker or No Drugs
VGL-Very Good Looking (Yuk!)

A quick way to screen ads is to mark the things that are important to you. First mark those with the preferred age; no sense wasting time on those who aren't in the age category you prefer. Then scan for other important details, such as; ethnic preferences, cultural or social interests, hobbies, and physical traits. Mark ads that seem compatible with your wants and desires.

Be sure to respond to ads that are congruous to your life-style. For example, if an ad reads: seeking someone who's wealthy and likes to travel. Don't respond unless those two qualifications truly apply to you. Rejection will only frustrate you, and you'll have wasted your time and theirs.

Answering an ad

Most ads are connected to 900 numbers, which always have a fee. Decide in advance how much money you're willing to spend. If you want to limit your spending, confine your telephone use to a specific time frame and pick only the best-matched ads.

Once you've screened the ads, you should have a number of them circled for further consideration. Decide which ones fall into the top ten. Find the mailbox number in the corner of the ad and jot down a brief description about the person, leaving room for further notes. For example: 8472-brown hair, brown eyes, likes to golf, wants someone with good sense-of-humor.

Before you dial the 900 number, have a reply ready. The advertiser will want to know some things about you too, so prepare a written summary. Include your first name, occupation, physical attributes, and hobbies, and if you'd like, what you're seeking in a relationship.

Once you've prepared a description of yourself, call the 900 number. You'll hear voice-mail instructions for answering an ad. After calling the advertiser, you'll hear the person's description. Write down their name, the qualities that interest you, as well as other notes such as, "left message," "enjoys sailing," or "sounds good." Then leave your prepared description. Make it brief and to the point— you're being charged by the minute. Leave key traits about yourself in a sincere manner. Don't be shy about stating your talents and interests, the advertiser needs some information to go on for his or her consideration about you. The better your description, the more replies you'll receive.

You'll generally know if you're interested, just by hearing someone's voice. Don't bother to listen to the message if their voice is a turnoff for you. Move on immediately so you don't waste your money.

Placing an ad

Some samples:

Left Brain Seeking Right Brain
Attractive, SBF, Brown/brown
5'6" 140 lb. 30's Prof.
Skg. attr. Prof. SBM
30-40 y.o. for fun activities and LTR.

Or

I Love Life but Need a Love Life
SJM, 5'10" 190 lb. Physician

Skg. attr. SJF, 25-35 for LTR
Enjoys the arts and fine dining

The headline is the hook. It's the phrase that will capture someone's attention.

You must stand apart from the competition. The better your headline the more responses you'll receive.

The actual physical placement of the ad is a consideration if you're given a choice. The beginning of the advertising section is read more than the middle or latter sections. The outer columns are read more than the mid-placed columns.

Many newspaper and/or magazines offer free dating ad space. The ads are usually positioned at the discretion of the publication. Because the ads are numerous, most people don't have time to read all of them. If you didn't receive as many responses as you'd have liked, it may have been because of the placement of the ad, rather than the headline. If however, the positioning was in a preferred spot, the headline may need to be adjusted. It's unlikely the content would've been a deterrent. The newspaper or magazine will help you with number of words, abbreviations, and wordage.

After you've written your ad, you'll be asked to leave a voice mail greeting. Prepare a greeting in advance, which should include some of the following:

Physical attributes: height, weight, hair color, eye color, age, ethnicity, general appearance.

Hobbies and interests: boating, bowling, music, dancing, etc.

Relationship preferences: honesty, sense-of-humor, short or long-term relationship, occupation, education, etc.

Leave your first name and a descriptive message. Be as concise as possible, the responder is paying for each minute and may not be willing to listen to a lengthy narration. Other things can be talked about later.

First-aid procedures for breaking the ice

On the call back, the ice will be broken very easily because you both received prior information about each other. You'll know within the first ten minutes whether you connect. If so, take the next step, and meet at a restaurant or coffeehouse.

Another reason that ads may be a stigma in our society is that it isn't the conventional way for people to meet. Normally you notice a person first and, if you're attracted, then you get to know them. Personal ads describe a person's basic personality and orientation. The encounter with actual appearance comes later.

The lack of spontaneity may seem awkward to some. Finding a blend of personal preferences, then deciding to go out on a date, is one step better than going on a simple blind date—something people have been doing for centuries! The pre-screening is merely an additional method to meet single people. You want to create dating momentum. Because . . . the more you date . . . the more you date.

Remedies and tips

1. Keep a positive attitude; don't take it personally if someone doesn't want to meet you. One never knows what motivates others. Maybe your voice is a reminder of a dis-

liked acquaintance; perhaps that person wants someone with a six-figure income or a perfect body (if it's mentioned); maybe he/she feels intimidated in some way. Don't spend time trying to guess what motivates others. It could be anything. Don't dwell on it, dismiss it immediately and think uplifting thoughts, call a friend, or distract yourself by watching a movie or going out.

2. Develop a polite way of saying no to people that you'd prefer not to see again. To reject or deny someone isn't easy. I find it best to say something such as, "It was nice meeting you, but I'd rather not continue." Or "It was nice meeting you, however, I don't think this is a match. Thanks anyway." Most people intuitively know when the chemistry isn't right and both say their farewells.

3. When answering or placing personal ads, be willing to meet lots of people. You won't be attracted to everyone you meet. In fact, you'll probably be attracted to only a few, but it only takes one.

4. You'll know within the first few seconds if you're physically attracted. If not, be kind and use your time wisely. Pick the persons' brain for business information, dating stories, or practice altruism by setting them up with a single friend or yours, if you think they'd get along.

5. Be discriminating with the periodicals in which you place or answer ads. Some ads contain sexual innuendoes, or the surrounding classified ads are for phone sex or escort services. The best newspapers or magazines are ones that appeal to the majorities and are more conservative with their advertising policies.

6. Try not to pre-judge, not everyone is gregarious. Some people are shy in crowds, and choose personal ads; a

one on one experience, as a less intimidating way to meet. You never know "who's who." The guy or gal you think may be a nerd, could be a knockout or a sweetheart.

7. If you have an intuitive feeling that someone is being insincere, or they sound unstable in some way, quickly move on and say good-bye.

8. You don't have to say you're a single. Tell others you merely prefer accompaniment. It takes away the "single" inference of a poor, pathetic, lonely person. When others know you simply prefer having a companion or friend, the stigma of being a single is lessened.

Resources

If leery of meeting unfamiliar persons, obtain a book called, *When In Doubt Check Him Out*, by Joseph J. Culligan, licensed private investigator. His book features many resources in which to check another's background.

Case studies

Joni, a marketing specialist, expected Mark, to be her prince because his response to her ad was so positive. Their phone conversation went smoothly. He was easy to talk to, successful, and she liked the sound of his voice. Mark was a banker and lived in a large home with a pool in the backyard. Joni loved to swim. She dreamed about the two of them; he being a tall, dark, handsome man, resembling Harrison Ford.

She envisioned the backyard filled with tropical plants and birds, picturing the two of them swimming in the evenings, sharing candlelight dinners on the veranda, in love and living in their own private paradise.

The day came when she met with Mark. He was tall all right (lanky,) dark (a black toupee,) and handsome (if you were nearsighted.) Although shocked at his appearance she was willing to overlook his physical characteristics. Mark and Joni tried to make their first meeting work because of the pleasant experience on the phone. They searched for similarities, but in the final analysis; had nothing in common, short of swimming.

The experience was actually a greater frustration for Joni than it should've been. Had she waited to find out who he really was, instead of fantasizing about who she hoped he'd be, she could have saved herself the disillusionment and disappointment brought on by her own expectations.

***

While talking to a guy named Bob, from the dating ads, I had the impression he wasn't very bright. His vocabulary seemed somewhat limited, and I judged him to be a simple man, but met with him nonetheless. As it turned out, he was astute, perceptive, and quick-witted. Our phone conversation had been his first attempt at asking for a date after a divorce; he was nervous and unsure of himself. It turned out my initial impression of him was incorrect. He was an entrepreneur; well traveled; well read; and had an appreciation of the arts. A far cry from the simpleton I'd originally thought him to be.

Here you have two sides of the same coin. One woman thought her date would be her dream man, while another thought hers to be her nightmare. A direct example of why preconceived notions need to be eliminated. Even though it's difficult.

***

Tim had gray hair, was tall, attractive, and a college professor. He met his wife Allyson—a pretty, petite brunette and interior designer, through the newspaper dating ads. He placed an ad stating he'd like a "jogging partner." She liked to jog and answered the ad. She and Tim were sexually attracted when they met, but they allowed a friendship to develop first.

They met for jogging on the beach, twice a week. She told me she stayed somewhat distant, because of the sexual attraction and knew if he recognized how intense it was for her, it might scare him away. This added mystery to her persona, which intrigued Tim. After a year, he asked her to marry him. They've been married for two years now, a cute and gracious couple, who generally recommend dating ads to their single friends.

***

My doctor, Lenny, a very intelligent gentleman, met his wife Susan, a gregarious, petite attorney, through the personals. They arranged to meet for coffee one night, were interested in one another, and dated from then on. Lenny informed me some of his colleagues paid hundreds of dollars to a matchmaker, and they still haven't found mates. Lenny and Susan recommend dating ads for meeting someone special.

Research and development for finding personal ads

Checking the Newspapers

Most newspapers have a personal ad section—from the larger periodicals, to the free local newspapers. These ads are usually located in the classifieds or the calendar section.

In addition, check your local supermarket, coffeehouse, or convenience market, which oftentimes carry miscellaneous periodicals with personal ads.

Bookstores

Find bookstores with a large magazine section, or newsstands that supply niche market items to find singles magazines.

Some singles magazine titles:
- *Single Solo Magazine*
- *Single Again Magazine*
- *Successful and Single Magazine*

These magazines have dating ads. You may write for a sample copy from the addresses provided below:

Living Solo Magazine
716 Ridge Place
Enid, OK 73701

Single Again Magazine
Circulation Dept.— Sholl and Assoc.
P.O. Box 3528
Fairfield, CA 94533

Successful and Single
129 Cabrillo # 201
Costa Mesa, CA 92627

Get Mental...Classes

Therapeutic attitudes

Stepping into a new zone

If you've taken classes in the past and haven't met anyone with whom to socialize or date, perhaps you didn't know what to say or, if you did, lacked courage to strike up a conversation. Perhaps you took a class with many married people, or weren't aware of any "unattached" students.

Take strides to leave your comfort zone and step instead, into a new, unfamiliar educational climate, by selecting classes you wouldn't normally attend. Make a poignant effort to meet people while you're there. Say and do things you ordinarily wouldn't do, and you'll most likely have a different result.

For Men

Getting into step in a new zone might entail taking a class that's generally abundant with women. Painting or cooking classes are good examples. Although many men excel in the art world, and numerous chefs are made, the majority in attendance is women.

Another consideration is one that promotes interaction. Writing classes are interactive when critiquing one another's work. This is especially advantageous for men, because women frequent writing classes more often than men do. My writing instructor, Irene can attest to that. Or, take a drama class, which is totally interactive.

For Women

Take a finance or auto repair class. Even though women do indeed invest and are astute in financial matters, and some understand mechanics to a degree; men commonly attend these classes.

If you're curious about data collecting, you might enroll in a statistics class, (now that would definitely have to be a requirement for credit if it were I), but the classroom is sure to be loaded with men! Exercising your brain, as you do your body, is known to prevent memory loss problems anyway. So, in addition to meeting the opposite sex, such classes are actually good for you.

***

Think of a class you wouldn't normally attend, and enroll. For instance, a local private college recently offered a class on Swimming with Dolphins off the coast of California in the Channel Islands. The class was taught by a former crew member of Jacques Cousteau's group. I'm sure you'd meet outgoing, adventurous people in such a class.

Prescription for where to go

Some typical coed classes:
- Accupressure or massage
- Advertising or marketing
- Art, such as: oil painting, water color, sculpture, or appreciation
- Astronomy
- Auto repair
- Computer
- Cooking
- Crafts
- Dance, such as: salsa, country-western, or swing
- Dating or relationship workshops
- Drama
- Financial planning or investing
- Flying lessons
- Foreign language
- Franchising
- Games: bridge, chess, black jack, etc.
- Gardening or horticulture
- History
- Home repair
- Liberal arts
- Math or statistics
- Media: radio, television, or movies
- Music: instruments, appreciation, or voice
- Photography
- Psychology
- Small Business
- Sports

- Woodworking
- Writing: fiction, nonfiction, or comedy

First-aid procedures for breaking the ice

Ask for help in the subject that you're studying, for example:

- "Would you be interested in starting a study group?"
- "Would you help me with this problem?"

Comment to someone in the class about their talent on the subject such as:

- "Judy, you're good at math—even without a calculator. Would you mind coming home with me to balance my checkbook?"
- "You made a great souffle Brian. Could you come to my house for a dinner party? My friends would love to taste your cooking."

Offer to help with someone else's homework by asserting:

- "If you'd like, I could help you with the assignment before class next week. How about meeting at the Upscale Coffeehouse downtown, before class?"

The class itself presents the common ground, which helps you to break the ice. Getting passed the "how do you do," stage is merely a matter of practice. Interact by speaking to people wherever you go. Rehearse with people—young or old, male or female—even children. Practice in elevators; comment on a good-looking tie or dress, try:

- "I like your tie, I always wonder where men get their ties . . .a gift from Santa, for fathers day. . .where did you get yours?"
- "That's a very pretty dress. My sister would love to have a dress like that for her birthday. Where did you get it?"

Speak up in grocery stores; ask the checkout clerk how she's doing, or comment on someone else's food items, such as:

- "It looks as if you're having a better dinner than mine tonight, I'd rather eat at your house."

I hear people say meeting others in a super market is the thing to do, yet have met very few who get dates at the grocery store. However, it's been done. Here are a couple of ideas on how to meet a man or woman this way.

The first way is to bump into another's cart and say:

- "Oops, sorry." And smile. You might add, "By the way, how do you like those cookies (in your basket)? I've been thinking about trying those."

Secondly, accidentally place your food items in their cart and say:

- "Oh, pardon me. Are you sure you don't want some of these delicious bananas?" (Or whatever the item may be.)

The more you practice speaking up, the easier it becomes. If you don't have a spontaneous wit, plan subjects to talk about ahead of time. Write down the topics and review them prior to the occasion. For instance, if you're taking a class that's food related; prepare to talk about recipes; favorite foods; or foods from another part of the country or the world. If you're taking a painting class, you might want to talk about museums, colors, or nature. If you're in a class related to engines, you could discuss models of cars, modes of transportation, or travel.

Remedies and tips

In one of my first writing classes we learned how to submit articles for publication. I learned a very valuable lesson about not "putting all of your eggs in one basket." We were taught to submit many query letters at a time, to increase the chances of a magazine accepting an article. Dating is just like that. By staying active, and showing up for many events, the odds of meeting people and getting dates are greater.

In addition, the teacher told us that by submitting different articles to many periodicals at one time, prevents us from focusing on one magazine too intensely.

Same with dating; doing many things with lots of different people deters us from concentrating only on one individual. Keeping busy; focusing on a variety of interests, allows dating relationships to unfold, as they will—without a busy mind interfering in the outcome. All you need do is show up for the next activity.

Case Study

Bruce, a geologist, met his wife Connie, an insurance agent, in a writing class. Bruce was delighted to find many more women than men in the class. He noticed Connie the first night. She was a tall, brunette, with brown eyes. During the semester they flirted by glancing and smiling at one another from across the room, but he was too nervous to approach. He had difficulty asking women for dates. He feared they'd be able to tell how awkward and fidgety he felt inside.

Bruce sensed the pressure to act on his interest as the semester was coming to a close. He knew he'd never see Connie again if he didn't do something. He finally bit the bullet, asked if she'd completed her story, and what she thought of the class. It turned out she was easy to talk to and felt relived. He immediately realized he wanted to know her better.

But just as before, on the last night of class, at the last minute, in the parking lot, right before she opened her car door to leave forever . . .he took a deep breath and said, "Let's go for some dessert and coffee." She hesitated before accepting. It had taken him so long to do what she thought should've been done weeks ago. However, she agreed to meet him at a local restaurant that evening.

Even though it took an entire semester for Connie and Bruce to get together, today, they have a successful and loving relationship. They've been married for seven years and have two children.

Research and development for finding a class

Bookstores and Libraries

Bookstores sometimes provide an area for reading groups, poetry readings, or classes on particular subjects.

The library carries local adult school and college catalogs. Ask the librarian where they're kept.

The Internet

To indicate searched-for words and data on the computer, put the associated words in quotes. The search vehicle will correlate the information. For example: "schools." Subject of interest . . . "drama." Name of your city . . . "New Orleans." State . . . "Louisiana."

Or, use an Internet directory by typing in you subject of interest. Try using: http://www.switchboard.com, or http://www.four11.com.

Utilizing the Phone Book

The **government** listings usually in the front of the White Pages section, lists state, county, or city colleges in your area. Colleges offer noncredit adult-school courses as well as classes for credit. In the same section, look up the city or county nearest you for the recreation department, senior or community center. Continue in the government section—under city— for high schools, which sometimes provide adult programs and activities.

The White Pages look under the name of your city for local high schools or the name of a private school with which you're familiar.

The Yellow Pages check the subject of interest, such as: airplanes, for flying lessons. Or, look under schools, where private and public schools are listed.

Retail shops

Occasionally retailers have information on classes. Try sporting goods stores; art supply stores; dance studios; night clubs; country clubs; ceramic stores; cooking supply stores; home improvement centers; martial arts studios; and shopping centers.

Start your own

Reading groups have become quite popular lately. Get a group of people together to read and discuss books. Try a writing, drama, cooking, or financial class in your own home by reviewing how-to-books, and/or rotate the location of classes in each other's homes.

The Newspaper

Your local or regional newspapers routinely offer listings of groups, workshops, classes, and the like, usually in the entertainment section of the paper. Check the newspaper weekly for interesting things to do.

Mailings

Just because something appears to be junk mail, it may not be "junk" after all. There could be an offering for a class or workshop in some of those paper piles. Also, sign up for any free singles publication mailings.

Treatment Plan Nine

Get Motivated...Parties and introductions

Therapeutic attitudes

Someone wants to meet you

Meeting new people is often difficult, even if the introduction is through a friend or family member. Sometimes our internal critic stops us from seeking introductions by saying things such as, "No one will want to meet me," "It's too uncomfortable to meet strangers," "What if I had a party and no one wanted to come?" or "All the good ones are taken." You're actually doing others a disservice by keeping yourself away from those who want to find someone to love—to find you. Know that somebody, somewhere, wants to meet you.

Our dark side would have us stay alone to wallow in self-indulgence and/or self-pity because it takes little effort to do nothing, or do only what's familiar. It's also a lonely, self-centered existence. Breaking through fear and maintaining a positive attitude is imperative for finding a mate. And

. . . if you had a party, I'm sure people would come. In fact, people don't have enough parties. Think of how it feels when you're invited to a party . . .elated that someone thought enough of you to invite you to join them.

One of the most common obstacles in meeting a mate is a poor attitude toward dating. Viewpoints ranging from: indifference to evasiveness, reluctance to bitterness, or apathy to dread, and so forth. A good attitude is clear of negative thoughts, you're able to think of yourself and others with care and concern. One of my heroes, M. Scott Peck M.D., describes attitude, in his book *The Road Less Traveled and Beyond* as, "One's acquired disposition or general approach of viewing things." When your attitude is positive you remove the barriers between yourself and others. By remaining good-hearted, not only do you meet a greater number, but a wider variety of people.

Decide to change your mind right now and conclude that you're worth fighting for, worth meeting, and valuable enough to do whatever it takes to meet someone special. Our self-esteem can rise with each small step we take for ourselves, even if it's simply making a decision to think a different way.

Prescription for where to go

Parties and introductions

Cures for what to do

1. Let your family and friends know you're interested in dating. Ask them if they know of any eligible men or women.

If so, there are a number of ways in which they might introduce you. First, have them give their friend your number, and your number to their friend, so that you may contact one another yourselves. Or, you might have a dinner at your home and invite your friends or family members, and their recommended guest over. Or, reverse it and have your friends or relations, invite you and their guest to dinner. Lastly, your "couple" friends could arrange to double date with you and their unmarried friend.

2. If you're a single parent, talk to other single parents to see if they have single friends and visa versa. You could swap baby-sitting nights with each other as you go out on dates with one another's friends or others.

3. Have a party. You invite five single people, and have each of your five friends bring a single person of the opposite sex; making sure the ratio of men to women will be even. (That is, if it's your preference.)

4. Swap dates as my friend Eileen and I do. She'll introduce me to men she's met in the past, and I'll introduce her to men that I no longer date. We have different inclinations toward men; she likes tall and assertive men; while I prefer average height and passionate; so we're easily able to do this.

5. Dating people from your workplace, with whom you interact on a daily basis, could be jeopardizing to your job if the relationship ends. Gossip or bitterness may lead to problems, so be careful when meeting people at work. However, there's not as great a risk when your co-workers introduce you to people from other areas of their lives, such as people they come into contact at work on an intermittent basis, for instance: outside vendors; consultants; temporary help;

lawyers; salespeople; speakers; insurance agents; or retirement and/or investment counselors. Or, perhaps they know of someone from their personal lives, where an introduction may be arranged.

6. Call up an old boyfriend or girlfriend. You never know their life circumstances at this very moment. It may be possible you're both single and available.

7. Often you'll see people in the office building in which you work such as in elevators, cafeterias, parking lots, the lobby, or restaurants. Flirt with them, or ask workers with whom you're familiar, if they know any of the prospects you have your eye on. If so and they're single, request an introduction. Find out from persons in other offices, with whom you know if they could acquaint you to any eligible men or women.

8. Ask for introductions from persons who have contact with the public. Hairdressers usually have a wealth of connections, especially with women. They know who's single and usually have the scoop on the lives and situations of many clientele. It would behoove any man to befriend a hairdresser. Lawyers have this sort of information on their clients also.

* * *

Taking risks in life, such as asking people for introductions, are acts of courage. The word courage stands for, *the state or quality of mind or spirit that enables one to face danger, fear, or vicissitudes with self-possession, confidence and resolution; bravery*. This is your life, live it to the fullest and, if someone doesn't like you, or doesn't want to go out

106

with you, it's just their unlucky day. Have the courage to stand up for what you want.

Resource

Listen to romantic music to keep the spirit of love alive in your heart. One of my favorite songs is *Have I Told You Lately*, by *Van Morrison*. Or, make a tape of all the songs that make you feel good.

Remedies and tips

Friends and acquaintances need to be reminded that you're in the market for meeting people. Keep all of your associates and contacts in mind when wanting introductions. That includes your doctor, the Avon lady, the pharmacist, your accountant, the librarian, your hairdresser, your lawyer, and anyone with whom you're on friendly terms. If you remind them, they'll usually remember. The squeaky wheel gets the grease is a cliche that continues through the ages, because it's tried, true, and it works. So squeak.

When asking for introductions, suggest they ask any of their single friends the following question: "How's your love life?" If the person responds, "I need one," Your friend might say, "Well, isn't that a coincidence . . . I just happen to know of a great girl (or guy) you might like to meet."

First-aid procedures for breaking the ice

When meeting new people through friends, relatives, or co-workers, the person that introduced you becomes your common link for breaking the ice.

To lessen anxiety when meeting with unfamiliar people of the opposite sex, act as if they're your same sex-friends. We aren't quite as judgmental of our same-sex companions. We don't think, what would my future be like with this person? We're not wondering about income level, or if they'd be a good lover.

By allowing friendliness, and not the projection of a "future mate" to be the focus, you're able to present a more casual demeanor. If you sense a special attraction for your new acquaintance, then you'll want to know more about the person's values and life-style but, until that day, a relaxed attitude will make you both feel more at ease.

Lastly, when wanting to break the ice at a party, bring a Polaroid camera with you. Take pictures of the guests. They're ready within a few minutes. Snap a picture of someone who appeals to you, hand them the photo and comment on the image in a complimentary fashion, "My, but you're looking simply marvelous darling."

Case studies

My friend Sheila is a marriage and family counselor who looks like Diane Keaton. She and I used to have parties with a core group of six single men and women, three males and three females. We'd ask the "core group" to invite one or two other single people to our parties. We called our group, The Dinner Club. Original name isn't it? The parties were theme based. We didn't want to concern ourselves with making idle chatter amongst people we were meeting for the first time. Some of the parties were as follows:

A Murder Mystery Dinner

One time we purchased a Murder Mystery Game and assigned ten people to play a different personality. Ahead of time, we mailed a "character description" to each guest, who then prepared to play the role of that particular personality the designated evening.

The murder setting and plot were described when the guests arrived. From there, we questioned one another to find out who was who, and where they were on the night of the murder.

After that, we sat at the dinner table to eat a delectable dinner, while continuing to gather information about each other's character.

When we finished dinner, it was time to solve the murder mystery. Each guest was asked who they thought had committed the murder and why. In the end, the murderer confessed—but not a soul guessed the killer. It was a disgrace I tell you, but a fun and easy way to become acquainted with new people. No "special connections" happened that night, yet everyone had great time.

A Movie Review Dinner Party

Another time, we invited The Dinner Club members and other guests for a buffet dinner and a movie. As we savored our tasty meal, guests were instructed to view the movie and be prepared to critique it afterwards. The criteria for analysis was based on content; message; acting; set; artistic style; and direction.

Once again, we weren't pressured into small talk. The critiques were outstanding, the opinions, passionate and compelling. Everyone participated. Ann, a nurse friend, and Jim, a pet therapist, were attracted to one another and dated a few times after that party.

* * *

Babbie and Mike met at one of our parties. This time we held a **<u>Question and Answer Dinner Party</u>**. A dinner was served and, soon after, we all gathered in front of the fireplace, in a crescent formation. Papers and pens were passed to everyone with instructions to write a question on it, fold it up, and place it into the basket. The questions were to be answered by each and every person. Questions such as:

- *What was one of your most embarrassing moments?*
- *Where did you go on your first date?*
- *What was one of the most daring things you've ever done?*
- *What was one of your best vacations?*

As each person took a turn answering, we laughed, booed, groaned, and were amazed at the stories. We learned a number of intriguing things about each other that night and had a blast.

Mike asked for Babbie's phone number that evening, and called her shortly after. They dated for about a year.

Get involved…Organizations and Associations

Therapeutic attitudes

The more you give of yourself, the more others give to you

Whether at a church gathering, the grocery store, or an association meeting . . . smiling, complementing someone, or voicing witty remarks to others projects a fun-loving attitude. And usually the response is returned in kind. Recently while in an ice cream store, the woman ahead of me ordered three banana splits. Knowing full well, the ice cream was not just for her, I jokingly said, "Don't you think you're overdoing it? Aren't you able to show a little restraint?" She laughed and answered, "Three banana splits is restraint!" Everyone cracked up. The atmosphere lightened up and spread throughout the store. When we give love, or in this case, a good laugh—joy, laughter, and love return to us tenfold.

One of the many forms of love is the giving one's time,

energy, or money, to an organization or association.

Although meeting men or women through an association or organization is relatively easy, it usually takes time to establish rapport and friendships. You may need to attend numerous meetings and functions before you even meet a single person. Then meeting one who's to your liking will also take time.

This isn't a "meat market" or dating service approach for uniting with available people. It's a more subtle way of meeting folks which takes it's own direction, in it's own time. At least that's been my experience.

By attending groups regularly, and interacting, people begin to trust and understand you. Once you've become a familiar friend, it's easier to mention you're single and would appreciate introductions to other single people. Of course, just because I'm saying this is a slow avenue for dating, you'll meet someone the moment you join.

Attending meetings at one organization to which I belong, has produced only three dates in a couple of years . . . pretty meager odds. I volunteer for many of the fund-raising events, but, since I have such a great time with these people, I stay—and have come to accept the fact that it isn't a wellspring for meeting single men. The male members are predominately married or out of my age range.

During those two years, my first date took place at a pool party. Ralph was a very attractive and nice high-school counselor, but extremely shy and fearful. It's surprising he managed to ask for a date at all.

I had a second date through an affiliate club where both organizations combined and convened at a social function. One of the members, Mary Beth, introduced me to Joel, a gerontologist. We had fun, but it wasn't a match.

Lastly, while master of ceremonies at a fund-raiser, I met the third gentleman, Chris—a member of the audience. He approached me after the show to ask me to dinner at a later date. Although a charming man, we had little in common.

Two years and three dates later is too long a wait to meet someone special, if you're diligent with the program I've laid out for you. It should take only one year or less to meet someone with whom you connect. I wouldn't advise you stay in an organization with such poor ratios unless you've joined for the contacts, or are passionate about the cause.

Prescription for where to go

Here's a list of organizations and associations for your consideration:

- Animal clubs or associations
- Automobile or other motor-vehicle clubs or associations
- Civic or community: historical societies, chambers of commerce, land preservations, and so forth
- College alumnus groups
- Hobby or avocation: astronomy, bird watching, cooking, etc.
- Political clubs or nonpartisan affiliations for the promotion of people or causes
- Professional groups associated with your vocation, groups for advancement of your career, or the changing of occupations

- Travel clubs: Club Med. for singles, or other similar organizations for single people

Philanthropic and/or cultural groups including fund-raisers such as:

- Animals: breeding, support, adoption, or cruelty prevention regarding all types of animals
- Cultural: art, science, theatre, or music; regarding any aspect; regionally, nationally, or worldwide
- Educational: mentoring, scholarships, for the academic development of people at any age, in any field
- Environment: air, water, or earth, for any aspect of environmental preservation—locally, regionally, or globally
- Health: aids, Alzheimer's disease, cancer, diabetes, multiple sclerosis, heart disease, organ donation, and so on
- Humanitarian: children, mental illness, hunger, family planning; to mention a few, whether locally, nationally, or worldwide

Cures for what to do

Choose clubs that will serve two purposes. First, that it's something you philosophically agree with and enjoy, and second, that it's coed. Most organizations will allow you to attend a few meetings before joining. Check the membership roster for the number of people and ratio of men to women in the club. Find out how many members regularly attend. There could be a seemingly even mix of men and women, but how many actually attend is often a different story.

For Women

Join organizations that interest men, such as business or science affiliations.

For Men

Join groups that bring in more women, as in philanthropic or creative endeavors.

First-aid procedures for breaking the ice

All of us know the benefits of feeling at ease when meeting new people. When in a social a setting, an excellent way to create relaxation with people is to offer information about you first. People will see you're willing to be friendly as you offer personal facts. For example, if you said: "Hi, I'm Catherine, I'm new to this group and I'd like to introduce myself. I've always been interested in this organization, but I didn't know how to contact you until reading an ad in the Sunday paper. How long has it been around?" This tells someone your name, that you're new and interested in the cause and, you read the newspaper.

Another way of handling conversation openers is to ask open-ended questions as: "Tell me about" . . . or "How did you" . . . For instance, "Would you tell me how this group originated?" or "How does the club raise money for the homeless?" These types of questions call for an explanation and open conversation easily. Avoid asking direct questions that would command a yes or a no answer as, "Do you come here every week?" or "Do you know most of the people here?" Asking direct questions may stifle ongoing conversation.

Bring business cards with you wherever you go. Hand them to association board members by stating you'd be interested in participating in future events. Give them to the person in charge of the mailing list. Keep them handy when meeting people wherever you go. Create some interesting personal or business cards with clever or unusual notations such as:

Andrea Mahoney PHD (<u>P</u>sychic <u>**Hair Dresser**</u>) No appointment needed, I already know when you need a haircut.

Mr. Randall Smith I specialize in Conditional Love. This card is good for one ice cream cone (but only if you eat it with me.)

A news director, named Rob, recently told me of a man in his late sixties named Morgan, who fabricated some business cards with his name and phone number on them, for his personal use. They read: **Professional Casserole Taster.** Rob said that lots of women invited Morgan over for casserole dinners because of those cards and soon after, the man remarried due to his clever wit and easy opener for a date.

Remedies and tips

Meeting strangers in an unfamiliar environment can create a certain degree of apprehension. To reduce anxiety, repeat the following affirmation, "I love people; I'm centered and confident; I'm here to help someone today." Affirmations are a way to reprogram your mind to think in a positive way—implanting a new perspective into your habitual thoughts. It isn't always easy, but by practicing this sort of self-talk, goodness soon becomes ingrained in your being, and you're able to cope more effectively. Or, if you prefer, you can talk to yourself, as I most often do, with humor. When I find my mind wandering to thoughts of fear or negativity, I say to myself . . . "Oh behave," in a voice intonation reflective of Austin Powers.

When we help somebody else, we tend to forget about our own worries and concerns. Focusing our attention on someone or something else provides an enriching and meaningful purpose for the activity ahead. Ask the host or hostess what you can do to help when at a meeting. Or reach out to the person who's sitting alone in the corner. Walk up to that person and introduce yourself.

Lastly, since life and people aren't perfect, interactions won't always go smoothly. I recall a time when I was talking with a man at a fund-raiser, who was extremely condescending . . . an awful experience. Luckily, I meet very few overtly rude people in my daily interactions. Because I'm not accustomed to such behavior, it caught me off guard. I stayed in the situation longer than was healthy for me. It would have behooved me to leave the moment his pompous attitude reared its ugly head.

Not only was I angry with him, but, I was angry with myself for staying in the conversation for so long.

I mention this circumstance because it depicts one of the more crude realities of life. And in order to protect your gentle spirit from the harshness of the world; and some of it's insulting, fear based members of our society; it's imperative you have a network of friends and family who support you through life's trials and tribulations. We all need people who are on our side; who'll listen to our struggles and successes.

Without a network of friends or family, dating risks can sometimes be too overwhelming to handle alone. If this were the case, your first step would be to reach out and make friends. Making new friends is easier than dating for two reasons. The first reason is that you aren't choosing a life-mate with whom you must live, day in and day out. Secondly, we humans have a tendency to favor people who like us and are flattered that someone wishes to be a friend.

It may sound silly for me to suggest forming friendships, but it's the basic foundation for acquiring the stamina and ability to do things that are difficult. Without love and support we wouldn't have a cushion to fall back on—to take the blows of a fall. When we know we're loved and cared for, we don't need the approval of strangers. Friends are people who are concerned for our well-being.

To make a new friend, call someone you like. Tell them how much you enjoy their company. Ask if they'd like to get together for lunch, or go to a ball game, and set a date and time. See if it's all right with them to call and talk. Joining a club or an association is a perfect setting for making friends.

Mentors

Kim, a thirty-eight-year-old woman, met Bonnie in an organization concerning women's issues. Bonnie was about fifty and, while in this women's therapy group, she frequently complained about having to say no to the many men who asked her out for dates each week. Bonnie felt uncomfortable turning men down.

After group one evening, Kim asked Bonnie to be her mentor. Bonnie seemed amused at her request and asked what Kim meant by mentor. Kim said she'd like to have the kind of problems Bonnie was having—attracting men and having to turn some down.

Kim felt shy meeting men. It had been a long time since her last relationship and was unsure of herself. Kim hoped that Bonnie could give her a few pointers. In turn, Kim could help Bonnie to say no to the men she didn't like. Bonnie loved the idea, and said she'd be delighted to be her mentor.

What Kim learned most from Bonnie weren't the things Bonnie said, but rather, the things she did. She observed that Bonnie truly liked men. She was a natural at flirting, and had a very sensual demeanor. Men could sense this in Bonnie and lingered near.

Kim realized that Bonnie had a winning attitude. She began thinking differently about men. Kim realized that men frightened her to some degree—due to some hurts from the past—and knew she needed to overcome her fear. She wanted to learn to love men just as Bonnie did.

Kim thought of other men in her life that she cared for, such as her brother and next door neighbor, and began to view most men in that light. She treated men as friends, until feeling comfortable around them felt natural. She oftentimes repeated the following phrase, "I love men, and men love me. I love men, and men love me." She'd say this to herself prior to going out at night and, as time progressed, it profoundly changed her point-of-view, until it finally became the truth.

As Kim came around to loving men, they were drawn to

her. It even changed her attitude toward people in general. She states that, "When you tell yourself how much you love people all the time; you end up loving people (almost) all the time. It's amazing how it works!"

Kim helped Bonnie also. Bonnie learned to say "no" more often. They supported one another and became good friends.

Resource

I recommend watching the old classic movie *Harvey*. James Stewart plays a most pleasant character. Observe his remarkably likable interactions with people and copy some of his behaviors. There's nothing wrong with imitating certain things people do. While performing as a stand up comic, we frequently rented tapes of our favorite comedians. We watched their actions and used the behaviors that helped draw the audience in.

Case studies

While working in the hospital, I had the privilege of assisting and supporting a couple named David and Diana, through a long and laborious delivery of their baby. We had plenty of time to talk between contractions.

David told me he met Diana at an astronomy convention in central California, where many astronomy clubs from across the country convened. David and Diana sat at the same table for a luncheon and lecture. They talked between breaks and were interested in one another, but they lived a hundred miles apart. They figured they were doomed to geographic undesirability and would never see each other again.

As fate or, in their case, the stars, would have it, they literally bumped into each other at the entrance of the convention center the next year. Sparks flew between them, the attraction so powerful, they chose not to separate. They spent the entirety of the convention together and, by the last day, knew they'd met their counterpart. They began to commute on weekends to be with each other. Their love grew and knowing that the commute was extremely arduous, David asked Diana to marry him. Diana sold her house, packed up her belongings, and married David. In addition, I'm happy to say that during my twelve-hour shift, they had a healthy baby boy.

* * *

A friend of mine named Gina, used to volunteer for the local symphony orchestra. She told me about a couple named John and Jan who met at one of these fund-raisers.

John, a business administrator, and Jan, a magazine editor, were both music lovers. They appreciated symphony music and enjoyed summer evenings under the stars while listening to Bach.

They'd previously, and independently, agreed to be the official greeters at the symphony, welcoming the guests and directing them to their seats. As John and Jan became acquainted and continually saw each other at ongoing events, John soon after, asked Jan out to dinner. He courted her and, according to Gina, they were married a few years later.

Research and development for finding organizations and associations

The Internet

For a large list of charities in the United States type: www.charities.org/homepage.html

An Internet directory is a great source for finding people and businesses, including, groups, associations, charities, and organizations. Go to: http://www.four11.com, or www.switchboard.com.

Libraries

Check the reference section of the library for The Gale Encyclopedia of Associations, a directory of associations across the United States.

The Newspaper

Your local newspaper is another good source for organizations and associations. Look in the calendar, business, or social sections for events.

Utilizing the Phone book

The Yellow Pages check under the topic headings of human services, social services, health service associations, clubs, organizations, or associations. Also look under topics of interest such as, art or music.

The White Pages check this section of the phone book if you know the formal name of the organization or association.

The government section has listings under state, county, or city organizations. Look up civic groups, or call city hall and ask for information on groups or organizations in town.

A few phone numbers and addresses of associations or organizations across the country:

Habitat for Humanity International
121 Habitat Street
Americus, GA 31709-3498
(912) 924-6935
Habitat for Humanity works in partnership with people in need, to build shelters that are sold to them for no profit through no-interest loans. The Web site address is www.habitat.org. Call for information, or to receive their newsletter.

The Humane Society of the United States
2100 L Street NW
Washington DC 20037
(202) 452-1100
This organization promotes public education for compassion for all creatures. Call for a newsletter or membership information.

Save the Children Federation
54 Wilton Rd.
Westport, CT 06880
(203) 221-4000

This agency assists children and their families in the U.S. and abroad to contribute to the growth of self-reliance. Call for information on program areas worldwide or in your district.

The International Chili Society
6755 Speedway Blvd.
Las Vegas, NV 89115
(877) 777-4427

Call for their newsletter or magazine. E-mail at: chiliics@ earthlink.net. A society for chili enthusiasts, who think, "chili is as American as apple pie." They sponsor chili cook-offs in search of the best chili and have world championship competitions. The Web site address: http:// www.chilicookoff. com

Toastmasters International
P.O. Box 9052
Mission Viejo, CA 92690
(949) 858-8255
Fax (949) 858-1207

This organization is nationwide. It's for men and women who wish to improve their communication and leadership skills. Call for a newsletter and/or directory.

American Council for the Arts
1 E. 53rd Street
New York, NY 10022-4415
(212) 245-4510

This is an advocacy group for the support and development of arts in America. Call for a newsletter or ask about a group in your area.

Amateur Astronomers Inc.
Union County Coll.
William Sperry Observatory
1033 Springfield Ave.
Cranford, NJ 07016
(908) 709-7520

The Web site address is: www.princeton.edu/georgel/aai.html. Call for a newsletter or to find out about meetings and conventions.

The New Orleans Jazz Club
Kernville, Texas
(210) 896-2285.

Call for a newsletter regarding current news of worldwide jazz affairs and activities.

Music for the Love of It
Berkley, California
(510) 654-9134

Call for their newsletter, which provides information on workshops, tours, and other data. This is an organization for recreational singers and music players.

Conservative Singles
Washington DC
(703) 821-5206.

Call for information and meetings.

Classical Music Lovers
Chicago, Illinois
(800) 233-CMLS
> Call for more information.

Singles for Charity
P.O. Box 93033
Rochester, NY 14692
> Write for more information.

Big Brother/Big Sister
1153 W. Fayette Street
Syracuse, NY 13204
> Write for more information.

Get Out. . .Singles events
(sponsored by the private or public sector)

Therapeutic attitudes

<u>Use the rule of three</u>

When you're looking for someone to date, use the rule of three, which means, date a man or woman three times before deciding if the two of you would or wouldn't be a match.

You're looking no doubt, for someone with integrity and character, who knows how to love. It's of great value to seek loving and companionable qualities, while matching your standard of living. Of course you won't know about a person until you spend time with them, but notice one's behavior, watching for signs of good character. Love is many things, but its primary qualities are those of kindness, compassion, tolerance, forgiveness, and honesty. How's that person treating others? Watch for actions more than listening to words. The cliche *talk is cheap* applies here.

By experimenting and dating different types of men or women—ones that may not be our typical picks—could turn out to be surprising. You may discover you're able to fall in love with some type you hadn't expected. It may be someone with whom a good friendship has developed, rather than one who had enticing sexual energy.

A friend named Linda—an attractive, petite, high school counselor—began an experiment by dating a few men she wouldn't normally date; such as those who appear to be "nerdy" or "boring." As time passed, she discovered some of these men had the qualities that were necessary for a lasting marriage: strong work ethics, loyalty, consideration, tolerance, appreciation, and honesty—all certainly admirable qualities for a partnership.

Linda said none of them had the persona of the charming, sexy, impressive men she'd normally date. Her new "experimental" men were either shy, not quite as debonair, nor were they as fashionable or as handsome as most. However, because Linda kept an open-mind, she ended up marrying one of the guys she thought she'd never date. Gene was a different ethnicity, kind, hard working, and loyal. She's come to learn and love new and important qualities she hadn't known in relationships before, and to her, he has become incredibly handsome.

Prescription for where to go

Singles events sponsored by the private or public sector

(Events sponsored by religious organizations are addressed in the chapter entitled, Religious or spiritual groups.)

These events may range anywhere from vacations to parties, including:

- Dances
- Vacations, tours, or cruises
- Sporting activities
- Dinners
- Parties
- Seminars and meetings
- Classes and workshops

Cures for what to do

Try several different singles events. Some groups will be right for you, some won't. Call in advance, to determine the age ranges and ratios of men to women, before you go. There have been times when, on my calendar, I've scheduled two singles events in one evening. If one were a dud, I tried another.

Also, try different types of activities such as: sporting events, parties, or dinners, rather than the typical singles dance.

First-aid procedures for breaking the ice

Learn something about somebody else. Have a "higher purpose," other than trying to get a date. Help someone feel less isolated, for example: if you see somebody, who looks apprehensive or nervous, introduce yourself. Engage in conversation.

Ask the person where they're from, or how he or she learned about the event. Ask that person if they know of other upcoming events. Offer information about yourself such as, "I know what you are thinking. How did someone whose ancestors were from Scotland and were such good bagpipe players, end up in a place like this?"

When you have "higher purposes," even helping someone to laugh, or groan, it can give the event and life more meaning. It can also get you more attention, which may lead to dates, because others see you're friendly and involved. However, if bagpipes aren't a topic of interest, speak of more common topics as movies, sports, or hobbies.

If you aren't warmly received, don't be discouraged. If someone isn't open to your company, it's possible that person is in a fearful state. They may be afraid of saying the wrong thing, or not wanting to be bothered. Perhaps you aren't the preconceived picture of the person they'd like to meet. On the other hand, they might have had a bad day at the office, or perchance it's a case of poor manners. It could be anything! If that person doesn't want to talk to you, quickly move on—next!

Resource

Dr. Gerald Jampolsky's book, *Love is Letting Go of Fear*, explains that at the root of, and in the nature of our being, are only two basic states of emotion: love or fear. An instructive and spiritual book that reminds us to stay in love with life. He presents this information with integrity, in an inspirational manner and, it's a quick read.

Remedies and tips

If you're generally uncomfortable at singles' affairs, give yourself a time limit. Two hours is a reasonable duration. You deserve a pat on the back just for getting out there and trying. Imagine if everyone hid away in his or her comfort zone, whether on the couch in front of the television or buried in a book. How would we ever meet one another?

Dr. Joyce Brothers wrote an article in the L. A. Times a few years ago, regarding social gatherings. She states, "Realize you are not alone. <u>Most</u> people consider themselves shy and uncomfortable for at least thirty minutes at a social event. After that time passes, you will usually begin to enjoy yourself more."

When we give in to the want to be comfortable all the time, we're actually stagnating. By going out to meet others, no matter how uncomfortable we feel, we've gone the extra mile with perseverance. Perseverance means, *steadfast singleness of purpose, as in the pursuit of a goal despite difficulties or obstacles*. These difficulties or obstacles could be any of the following:

- The extra energy it takes to find others to date.
- The numerous types of people we must meet before we find one with whom we're compatible.
- The money it takes to socialize.
- The frustration we may feel when disappointments or rejections arise.
- The self-defeating thoughts we think that keep us from extending ourselves or being our best.

You may have a common dilemma; staying in a relationship that isn't right for you, because leaving it would mean feeling the pain of loss and loneliness; then having to face the arduous task of socializing to meet and date others.

I've done this. There were times when I'd become weary—trying to find my soul mate, so I stopped to rest with someone I knew wasn't the best choice for me, and visa-versa. The danger comes in to play when one begins fooling oneself—convinced that this was what they really wanted. When the relationship ends, either or both are shocked that it didn't work out. By realizing there are times we just need to rest with another, we can allow ourselves to do that or forgive ourselves if need be, and move forward.

More remedies and tips

Here comes the judge

Our perspective on the world is all in the way that we interpret it. For example, if we see a magic show as an event where someone tries to fool us and we're unable to figure out the tricks, perhaps frustration will result from the deception. In which case, we'd most likely not want to go to a magic show again. However, if we view a magic act as an entertaining and clever event, and stop trying to figure it out, we can relax and enjoy it, making it more likely that we'll do it again.

The same goes for singles events. If we see them as affairs filled with a room full of losers—a place catering to the socially impaired—we may not want to attend. However, if someone as wonderful as yourself is there; could it be that another person, just as awesome as you might be there too? Remember that it takes only one other person to make a match. By taking a positive view, we become open to participating in a wider variety of events, and end up with more opportunities to meet people.

The reliability of singles events rids you of the guesswork as to whether someone is available for dating.

Your willingness to participate in numerous pastime activities is the secret to meeting a match. The more you take part, the more you increase your odds for meeting someone special. The more you increase your odds, the sooner you'll be a couple.

Case study

Patrick, an art dealer, met Debra, a cute blonde and a graphic artist, at a progressive dinner and dance. This is where the women stay seated during the entire dinner and the men change tables after each course.

Patrick was drawn to Debra, after a conversation with her during the dessert phase of the dinner. He thought her to be very attractive and bright. He asked her to dance afterwards and, before she left, he asked for her number. She wasn't going to give it to him because she didn't like his physical appearance. His short stature and baldness didn't meet up with her tall, dark, and handsome expectations.

Because of Debra's five-foot-five inch height and hourglass figure, I feel sure she'd dated lots of good-looking men through the years. She had recently terminated a tumultuous relationship—with a tall, dark, and handsome salesman. So, prior to leaving for the dinner that night, she remembered a promise she made to herself— that she needed to get out and date, whether the men were fat, bald, or had acne. So she gave him her number, he called and a few evenings later and they went out.

To Debra's surprise, Patrick was extremely witty. As she learned more about him, she found he was a whiz in business and had a sweet, loving demeanor. His kindness, combined with his intellect, sense of humor, and generous nature, were the traits reflective of the sort of person she respected.

Debra hadn't believed she could love a short, bald man, yet she did. Using her old approach, she wouldn't have picked him in a thousand years. Since she decided to date all kinds of men, she now has a wonderful partner who'd do anything for her.

Research and development for finding singles events

<u>The Internet</u>

There's much information regarding singles events on the Internet. Here are only some of the addresses:
- www.singlesmall.com
- www.cupidnet.com
- www.parentswithoutpartners.com
- www.datecentral.com
- www.singlesonline.com
- www.singlesite.com

These are fabulous sites for cutting-edge information about dating and meeting others. More detailed dating via the Internet in the chapter entitled, Get High-tech.

Internet travel sites

You needn't wait for a significant other before you travel. You could meet someone while on vacation, especially with a singles travel group. Try:

- www.cupidnet.com/trvlsits.html
- www.singlesworld.com/mission.htm
- http://www.thejewishpeople.org./jsc/travelintro.html
- www.singlestravel.com

Look in an Internet address directory for names of social groups or travel groups at the following directory Web sites: http://www.four11.com, http://www.switchboard.com , or http://www.yellow-page.com. Or, call you favorite travel agent.

The Newspaper

The best resource for finding singles events can be found in the entertainment or life-style sections of the newspaper. The Thursday or Friday editions have listings of singles events for the upcoming weekend.

Sometimes free, local newspapers advertise singles events. And, some coffeehouses have newspaper stands that carry local publications.

Magazines

Check newsstands and magazine racks that carry a large variety of publications.

A few titles you may want to check:

Single Again Magazine—For divorced, separated, or widowed single people.

Successful and Single—Distributed in Orange, Los Angeles and San Diego Counties. It focuses on dating and single living situations.

Living Solo Magazine—Information on dating and covers many topics expressly for single people.

Metrolina Singles—A singles magazine for residents of North and South Carolina.

All of these magazines pertain to single people everywhere. Some are more geographically specific regarding events and dating ads. To obtain one of these magazines write to the following addresses for a sample copy or subscription:

Successful and Single
170 E 17th St. Suite 212
Costa Mesa, CA 92627
(949) 645-4811
Call or write for a sample copy.

Single Again Magazine
Circulation Dept.— Sholl and Assoc.
P.O. Box 3528
Fairfield, CA 94533
Write for a sample copy.

Living Solo Magazine
716 Ridge Place
Enid, OK 73701
Write for a sample copy.

Metrolina Singles
800 Briarcreek Rd. Suite DD-518
Charlotte, NC 28205
(704) 375-5181
Call or write for a sample copy.

Networking

Ask all of the single people you know where they go to meet people.

Travel Agents

Use your local travel agent for information on singles-travel information. Or call:
Singles Travel Network
(888) 237-6080

Singles Parties, Affairs, and Dances

In Orange County CA, there's a singles group called Parties Etc. by Mimi Fane. She sponsors singles events such as, dances in hotels or progressive dinners in restaurants. All of her clientele are through word of mouth. Her number is (714) 731-3399.

I've recently come across a fairly new group that's trying to get away from the bad rap of "singles groups." It's an assemble of people who get together to do all sorts of things, that just happen to be single, called Adventure Fun Addicts. The emphasis is on fun, not dating. The recorded information line is: (714) 647-7723. The office number is (949) 660-7976.

Start Your Own

Order *Parties For Fun or For Profit* from Social Lite Productions or use some of the ideas from Treatment Plan Nine for party ideas.

Below, I've listed more singles groups around the country:

Selective Singles Social Club
Chicago, Illinois
(312) 631-4263

Tall Clubs Int'l.
N. Hayden #C-108
Scottsdale, AZ 85257
(800) 521-2512

This is a national group that has associations all over the country. Call to see if they have one in your area.

New England Singles Network
Cambridge, MA
(617) 259-1118

The Single Life
Waltham, MA
(800) 294-9996

Spring Singles Weekend
Flint, MI 48503
(313) 238-2631

National Singles Round Up
P.O. Box 75
Driscoll, ND 58532
(701) 387-4466

South Jersey Single Professionals
Trenton, NJ"(609) 429-4553

Seashore Singles
Trenton, NJ
(609) 779-7884

Singletons
Kings Lane
Rochester, NY 14617
(716) 266-8192

30 and Holding
Williamsville, NY
(716) 634-3010

Umbrella Singles
P.O. Box 157
Woodbourne, NY 12788
(914) 434-6871

Over 40 Club
Philadelphia, PA
(610) 337-3682

Select Singles
Philadelphia, PA
(610) 527-4642

Tall Singles- The Tower Club of Phila.
Philadelphia, PA
(610) 848-7881

Get High Tech...Internet dating

Therapeutic Attitudes

Does your love life need CPR?

Revive your love life by using the Internet. Presently, men use the Internet more than women, but this is rapidly changing. Internet dating can be the answer to finding a companion. The CPR in your love life might just be a product of a computer search, as you Capture Perfect Romance.

Some people are fearful of using the Internet as a means of dating because the mode of communication is limited to a typed message, and the viewing of a picture. This might restrict the ability to gauge one's integrity, character, and background. But how well do we really know others through any avenues of dating?

Furthermore, you don't have to place yourself in jeopardy. Safeguards are available when utilizing the Internet for dating purposes.

Obtain relationship support and advice in chat rooms. Some are designed exclusively for people to interact by typing messages to one another in regards to dating and relationships, where you'll receive advice.

- A bulletin board is a variation of a chat room, only the partaker relates a question in reference to dating or relationships, and others will respond by posting advice or stories of a similar nature in response to questions.
- An Internet service has been designed specifically for checking a person's background, called Datesmart, at: http://www.datesmart.com. Or call them at: (888) 84-CHECK. Datesmart will check a person's history for aliases, criminal background, divorce and marriage authentication, in addition to verifying other segments of lifestyle.

Prescription for where to go

Internet Dating

Singles' sites available on the Internet include:
- Bookstores
- Chat rooms
- Dating services
- Malls
- Matchmakers
- Personal advertising

Cures for what to do

An overview of the singles' data above:

Bookstores

Most people are aware of the availability of purchasing books through retailers on Internet sites, where a wide variety of books on the subject of dating and relationships can be found. Book sites are found in singles' malls, on various authors' Web sites, on publishers' Web sites, or through retail Internet bookstores. Some addresses are provided at the end of the chapter.

Chat rooms

You can instantly communicate with people by typing messages back and forth. This is called chatting. Chat rooms for dating and relationships are available through some of the singles' sites, itemized at the end of the chapter.

Dating Services

Dating services furnish you with information on other single men or women, all seeking to date, mostly by way of personal ads. There's usually a charge to become a member of a dating service.

Malls

Malls are a cluster of Web sites where you may chat, shop, and /or obtain materials or information for singles. You might find: books; bulletin boards; magazines; chat rooms; singles events; ticket sales; newsletters; and activities.

Matchmakers

Matchmakers' set-up dates for you. They collect data about yourself and what you want in a mate, then match your qualities and desires to another's profile of similar compatibility. The rates vary.

Personal Advertising

Ads are placed with data such as: first name; age; height; weight; interests; and ideals you seek in a relationship.

Unlike newspaper ads, Internet advertising sites contain photographs. Although, supplying a photograph is not required, it's highly suggested. You have better odds of attracting someone when they know how you look. The responses tend to increase when they can see you.

If you don't know how to post your picture on-line or have a scanner, there's a company called Seattle Film Works that provides film made for computer imaging. The film will fit into any 35mm camera. Have someone take your picture with this film, then mail it back to Seattle Film Works, where they develop, digitize, and compress it onto a floppy disc. In addition, you'll receive not only the floppy, but also prints, with up to 36 photographs per roll. From the floppy, you'll be able to download your picture to the dating ad.

To reach Seattle Film Works phone:
 (800) FILMWORKS
E-mail at info@filmworks.com.
Or visit their Web site:
http://www.filmworks.com

Once you've <u>placed</u> your ad, the service will provide an e-mail address where people may respond.

To <u>answer</u> an advertisement, you'll e-mail a message to that person—along with data about yourself—by using: your first name only; your phone number or e-mail address; and a brief description of yourself. When answering ads, the advertiser will want to see your picture also, so be prepared to provide one.

Before joining a singles dating service on-line, you may want to know:

- How many members live nearby?
- Are they in your preferred age range?
- How many clients belonging to the service?
- Do they provide background checks?

Most services will furnish information regarding company policy before you're required to pay. If not, you may want to try another service.

When meeting blind dates, make sure to meet in a public place—don't allow anyone come to your residence until you know him or her better.

Remedies and tips

When in chat rooms or other forums for Internet communication, be careful not to fall in love with idyllic thoughts and words typed by another. Many are tempted to conjure up romantic illusions as to whom the typist could be.

For example, I've created fantasies about men, when answering dating ads. As I talked to someone I believed to be a great guy, I'd imagine he was as handsome as a movie star,

145

and rich as an Insurance HMO CEO.

Reality hit when after meeting him, I found he was as bald as an eagle, with thin strands of dyed hair swooped across the top of his head, wearing coke-bottle horn-rimmed glasses, donning a white wrinkled shirt, and polyester pants.

A few men have had the same kind of experience, only a female variation. Here's one of my favorite stories told to me by a man named Mark, who used personal ads. His prospective date, Sandra, described herself as being average height and weight, attractive, open-minded, with a strong work ethic. She told him she was an artist and had a studio.

He expected to meet an interesting and pretty woman, talented in the fine arts and he could picture the two of them attending art shows on Sunday afternoons. When they met, she was attractive all right, if you wanted a female wrestler. He found that her open-mindedness referred to her being open to wearing tattoos, because she owned and operated a tattoo parlor—some artist. She departed on a motorcycle. The poor man wouldn't have a blind date for years afterwards. Luckily, he came around to realizing his experience was truly an aberration, and tried it again with better results.

Resource

If you're having trouble accepting "singlehood," read *God on a Harley*, by Joan Brady. It's a wonderful spiritual tale about loving your life, staying in the moment, and doing the things you love to do.

Case studies

I met Jack at a spiritual retreat. He told me that he'd met his wife Mary in a chat room. At first I cringed, wondering if it had been an "unmentionable" chat room, but was relieved to hear it was a chat room for musicians.

She's a pianist—he plays the saxophone. They discovered that not only did they live in the same county, but were the same age, single, and so delved into typing to one another with vigorous enthusiasm. Jack asked Mary to meet him for coffee soon after.

Never in a million years had he expected to meet and marry the love of his life in a chat room. He said he was astonished because, not only were they passionate with music, but they felt chemistry between them the moment they met. Jack says he always recommends the Internet to single people.

***

I took a Web site design class recently, and during the course, the instructor, Cleo, told us about a student of his, a single woman in her late sixties, Doris, who designed a Web site for herself. Being new to the area, she wanted to make friends. The site featured pictures of her performing line-dancing and playing bridge. An e-mail address was provided for others to contact her and, believe it or not, within weeks she'd made lots of friends, not only with men, but also with many women. Because of her Web site, she made contact with Mr. Right and remarried within the year.

***

Gary, a computer programmer, met his girlfriend Marcia, a flight attendant, on an on-line dating site. Gary says people who use computers are most often professionals, they're usually smart and have active lives. He contends that quality people have a good chance of meeting this way.

After his first attempt at Internet dating, he received ten responses the first week, and at least five more replies for weeks thereafter. However, now that he's met Marcia, he's taken his site down—but says it's a great way to get dates.

Research and development for finding Internet dating sites

Explore some of the following Internet addresses:
- *www.singlesonline.com* Singles on Line
- *www.cupidnet.com* Cupids Network
- *ww.datecentral.com/* Date Central
- *www.singlesites.com* Single sites
- *www.as.org* American Singles
- http://www.love.aol.com Love@AOL
- *www.match.com* Match
- *www.webpersonals.com* Web Personals
- *www.singlec.com* Single Christian Network
- *www.singlesmall.com* Singles Mall
- *http://www.find-a-mate.com/* Find a Mate
- *http://www.one-and-only.com* One and only Yahoo personal ads

Other ways of finding information on the World Wide

Web are by searching the Internet by typing in key words such as: "singles," "dating," "romance," "matchmaking," "relationships," and/or "love."

Create your own Web page

Here are a few addresses:

* http://www.webwizard.moreprofits.com/ Web wizard
* http://www.myezpage.com/ My e z page
* www.webondemand.net/ Web on demand

A word of caution

Regarding the use of photographs on-line, anyone can take them and put them up wherever they want. It could be your face on someone else's body etc.— just be aware.

Also, certain people who use the services have been known to abduct innocent people by luring them with promises of love and money. Promises they'll never keep. Don't travel out of your area to meet people. If you suspect malicious goings on, report it to the proper authorities.

Get Intellectual. . .Lectures and Seminars

Therapeutic attitudes

Opposites attract

It may benefit you greatly to attend lectures and seminars. Wherever more than a few people congregate, for the benefit of improving themselves, there's a potential for meeting someone special. People who are into self-improvement, may have the capability of maintaining a full, long-lasting relationship, because they care about the quality of their lives.

Women ought to attend lectures on subjects that normally arouse men's interests, such as, finance seminars, computer information, career development, and the like.

Men would benefit from going to seminars women frequent, such as, personal growth seminars, culinary programs, or the arts.

By attending a lecture on a subject you wouldn't normally pursue, you'll open the door to the people you wouldn't ordinarily meet.

Spiritual seminars have become very popular lately. Many interesting people are looking to improve themselves in this area. If you have a personal interest in spiritual matters, you have a good chance of meeting someone with whom you have something in common, in an important area of your life.

Prescription for where to go

Lectures and Seminars

Lectures or seminars can range from one-hour long to a weekend. Some topics of interest:
- Architectural topics
- Art lectures
- Authors' lectures
- Communications topics
- Culinary related subjects
- Financial planning
- History lectures
- Job or career related lectures or seminars
- Museum lectures
- Nature lectures
- Personal growth or motivational seminars
- Relationship seminars
- Science lectures or seminars
- Spiritual topics
- Travel lectures

Cures for what to do

When sitting next to someone at a lecture or seminar introduce yourself and talk to him or her. Chatting with people next to you breaks the tension of being among strangers and may create a more relaxed atmosphere. It's a friendly gesture, as well as an act of courage on your part.

Many people won't speak up when around those with whom they're unacquainted for fear of rejection or appearing foolish. It would be tragic to look back on your life and realize you didn't fully live because you were afraid of appearing the fool rather than trying something new, regardless of success or failure. Besides, flops are only learning experiences.

Since most people understand that no one is perfect, even an awkward remark can be endearing. It sometimes brings us closer to others, because it gives us permission to flub-up also. Some of America's favorite personalities are those who are able to laugh at themselves, who aren't afraid to act the fool or play a clown. Steve Martin, Joan Rivers, Mike Meyers, or Damon Wayans are good examples.

Remedies and Tips

Get to know all types of people, even if someone is out of your age range, or the people next to you are a couple. Someone may have a connection for you on down the road. They might know people, who could connect you to a new line of work, a vacation getaway, or a creative endeavor; which would lead you to a new realm of acquaintances. I once met an older woman, Jo, at a medical seminar who had seven sons. One of her sons, Richard, was divorced and had no special girlfriend at the time. Later, she introduced me to him and we dated for awhile.

First-aid procedures for breaking the ice

During breaks in the seminar or lecture, tell a witticism or prized story. Here's a clever joke told by a comedian named Jim Hope. While performing at a local comedy club, he wrote a joke strictly for The Improv, located near the University of California, in Irvine, "Gee, driving here tonight, I had to take Stanford Ave., to Harvard Pl., to University Dr., I didn't think my I.Q. was high enough to be here."

Or, ask two people to lunch or coffee. Give two people your business card and ask two other people for theirs. Promise to start a conversation with at least three new people. Ask someone to take a walk at the break. Ask another to join you for lunch.

To begin conversations with strangers, speak of common topics.

General topics for conversation

Conversations for the Season
- Have you taken any trips or vacations this summer?
- Do you like to snow ski?
- How was your summer?
- Have you been to New England in the fall?

Cultural Questions

- What sort of music do you like?
- Are you reading any good books?
- Which authors do you like?
- Have you seen the Van Gogh exhibit?

Topical Conversation

- Have you seen the movie Saving Private Ryan?
- Have you been to the Too Good to be True restaurant?
- Are you on the Internet? Do you know of any interesting sites?
- How did you find out about this lecture or seminar?

Once you've detected a mutual interest in a topic, then encourage the other person to tell you more about his or her thoughts on the subject.

If you find you're interested in someone, then you may want to get more personal by asking some of the following questions:

- Where were you born or raised?
- Where do you live?
- What do you do for a living?
- What do you do in your spare time?
- Do you have any brothers or sisters?
- Does your family live nearby?
- Do you belong to any organizations or clubs?
- What do you think you'll be doing one year from now?
- What do you think you'll be doing five years from now?

Case studies

One of my fellow team members, Tammy, told me how she'd met her husband Jeff, a paramedic. They sat next to one another in class during a lecture on respiratory distress at the hospital and became acquainted.

Tammy, a new employee at the hospital, had seen Jeff in the Emergency Department where she worked. However, they always noticed one another but couldn't start a conversation because they were too busy.

Jeff caught a glimpse of Tammy in the respiratory class and deliberately sat next to her. An immediate friendship developed. They talked to one another at the lecture breaks and continued to talk at every opportunity while working in the Emergency Room. As they came to know each other better, the attraction grew stronger.

Tammy had prepaid for a hike and camping retreat in the mountains, and when Jeff asked Tammy what plans she had that weekend, she told him about hiking in the mountains and asked him if he'd like to come along. He'd planned to ask her out anyway, so he went. Tammy told me that those two days in the mountains; hiking; sleeping under the stars; and sharing nature together; secured their feelings of love and deep affection. They married a year later.

* * *

Vera, an assistant administrator at a medical center, met a captivating man, named Ryan, through a finance seminar for raising venture capital. The room was packed with

156

men. Vera said that attending such an event provided a great way to meet talented, interesting, and ambitious people.

Ryan enrolled in the seminar because he was contemplating a franchise purchase. As they talked between breaks, Vera mentioned her upcoming singing audition for South Pacific at a local theatre group the next day. To her surprise, she discovered Ryan was a pianist. He asked her if she'd like to practice some songs after the seminar. He played beautifully, and assisted Vera in rehearsing songs. They had a wonderful time together, but lived too far away to pursue a relationship. However, and more than likely, thanks to Ryan, Vera got the part. Had she not gone to the seminar, and taken a few risks, she wouldn't have had the experience, nor would she have achieved the role as the head nurse in South Pacific.

Research and development for finding lectures and seminars

The Newspaper

Your local newspaper provides a good source of seminar and lecture schedules. Look in the entertainment or lifestyle sections of the Thursday or Friday editions.

Free regional newspapers also regularly announce events.

* * *

I found the most interesting nature program in the entertainment section of the newspaper. The event was listed as an "Owl and Bat Hike" at the Mission Viejo Land

157

Conservancy. I called for reservations and rounded up a couple of adventurous nurses, named Patty and Gina, to come along.

We attended a lecture on bats, prior to the hike. After that, the group gathered in the Wilderness Park on our search for owls and bats. We used sonic finders to locate the bats. We sighted only one owl, but detected more bats than the specialist had seen all season. It was exhilarating.

The nature hike presented a wholesome way to meet people. Unfortunately, the only men in attendance were either married or under twelve. But we had a blast, out in the woods, in the dark, learning things about creatures of the night. If you're interested in contacting The Rancho Mission Viejo Land Conservancy in San Juan Capistrano, California, call: (949) 489-9778.

Trade journals or newsletters

The trade journals in your profession often have upcoming events published in their magazines or newsletters. Subscribe to trade newsletters or journals to find lectures and seminars. Check the Oxbridge Directory of Newsletters at the library.

Churches

Check flyers or bulletins at church services, or call one of your favorite churches or synagogues about possible upcoming lectures and seminars.

***

One of my favorite spots for retreats and lecture series' on spiritual matters is held in Santa Barbara, CA, at a place called:

La Casa De Maria
800 Bosque Road
Santa Barbara, CA 93108
(805) 969-5031.

It's a nonprofit retreat and conference center of Christian origin, governed by a multi-denominational board of trustees. A few of the many program titles:

- *The Spirituality of Relationships*
- Dreams and Inner Healing
- Living Wisely and Well
- *Renewal for the Work Weary Soul*

The programs change periodically and they're always interesting.

Libraries

Examine bulletin boards or look for flyers on upcoming local activities. Check the Oxbridge Directory of Newsletters, located in the reference section of the library. This directory has thousands of entries of newsletters from any and every subject you can think of.

The Internet

Type in key words with quotations around them, such as: "lectures," "seminars," or "events," along with the subject you're interested in, say, "literature" or "art," then type in your city, county, or state, for the location nearest you. It would look like this: "seminars," "relationships," "Chicago." Or, try: "Seminars, relationships, Chicago."

Bookstores

Quite a few bookstores offer lectures by authors or author representatives, and have flyers at the counter. Or, find a bookstore that carries a large selection of magazines or trade journals. Try Borders bookstores. Borders is a cutting edge, innovative bookstore. The Web site address is: http://www.borders.com/

Schools

Adult schools usually offer lectures, tours, and seminars. Call your local school district for an adult-education catalog.

Museums

Frequently, museums have tours or lectures. Here are some popular ones:

Smithsonian Institute
S I Building, Room 153
Washington DC 20560 - 0010
(202) 357-2700

Armand Hammer Museum
10889 Wilshire Blvd.
Los Angeles, CA
(310) 443-7000

American Museum of Natural History
79th Street & Central Park W
New York, NY
(212) 769-5800

Museum of Science and Industry
5700 S. Lake Shore Dr.
Chicago, IL
(773) 684-1414

American Museum of Natural History
79th Street & Central Park W
New York, NY
(212) 769-5800

Get inspired. . .Religious or spiritual groups

Therapeutic attitudes

<u>Church chat</u>

When attending any function of interest to you, you'll probably speak to, and meet, others of who have a similar perspective on life. This is expressly true of religious or spiritual groups. When you meet a person in a harmonious environment, chances are . . . your congruous beliefs will help form a comfortable relationship because you'll have a code of ethics related to spiritually principled living. When both are following similar belief systems, we understand one another better, and we have a foundation for a successful relationship.

Prescription plan for where to go

Religious and spiritual groups

Most have singles' groups. Some types of gatherings:
- Dances
- Dating services

- Dining
- Discussion groups
- Lectures and seminars
- Outings
- Retreats
- Sports activities
- Study groups
- Support groups

Cures for what to do

Try several different groups to find one that's compatible with your ideology. If you've not determined a denominational preference, try various religions or philosophies to see what others believe.

Establish your presence in a group by regularly volunteering to help—whether it be greeting people, working in the bookstore, or handing out flyers.

Think of yourself as an actor or actress. Pretend you're playing the part of Ghandi, or a "guru of goodwill." Tell yourself you'll choose a couple of people with whom to be absolutely gracious. Ask if they'd like a cup of coffee or glass of water. Tell them something you like about them, such as the tone of their voice, their clothing, or their choice of words. Ask those same people for their opinion about the sermon, the lecture, or the subject matter. Listen without disruption.

One of the most inherent desires in human beings is to be heard and understood. What better way to be a living example of selflessness than to listen without disruption? Having a role to play gives us a more active purpose in the participation of any event and, gives us a focus.

As you demonstrate loving, kind acts—others will gravitate to you. And who knows . . . someone may be interested in becoming better acquainted with you.

First-aid procedures for breaking the ice

Introduce yourself to a few other people and ask questions such as, "Hi, my name is Meghan. I'm new and I'd like to get to know some new people. Are you a member? How did you find out about this church/synagogue? Do you come every week? What sort of activities does this organization offer?"

Rarely expect others to extend themselves to you. You make the first move by introducing yourself and offering greetings. This is one of the timeless secrets for winning friends. Presenting a handshake is actively taking part in meeting others. Life gets easier when you take charge of your life in this way. You aren't passively allowing life to dish out whatever comes along.

Remedies and t,

If feeling unwelcome, or that you don't belong in a certain group, go with your instincts and find a new place. Be true to yourself and find a place where you fit in, and don't stop until you find the right group. Sometimes it takes many attempts to discover the spiritual ideology where you feel you can best relate, coupled with the right mix of people.

When going to many new and unfamiliar places. It helps to repeat affirmations to yourself such as, "Today I'll trust that God's will is working in and through me. I let go of all worry and concern. I'm relaxed and meet new people with ease." Say it over and over as you drive to any destination. By repeating affirmations enough, the belief becomes a reality.

Resource

Read anything by Emmet Fox. He writes solid spiritual and inspirational books such as: *Around the Year with Emmett Fox* or *Find and Use Your Inner Power*. His books are helpful for the continuance of building inner strength. An active social life is filled with risks and, takes energy. His books will motivate you to remain persistent in keeping the faith to reach your goals.

Case study

I met Janet, an advertising executive, at a Christian singles dance. As we talked, she admitted she came routinely, in hopes that Brad, a handsome man she met at the dance awhile back, would come again. She'd also seen him at the singles' church services. Janet described him to me in detail.

The very next weekend as I attended the dance once more—I noticed Janet. There she was, dancing with Brad. He looked just as she'd described. They danced all evening. I took note of the way she interacted with him. She dressed in a form-fitting skirt and blouse, smiled often, and paid close attention to him. She'd known they'd make an exceptional match and she was correct. A few months later, I saw them seated at the regular church service, as a couple. Janet was persistent and her patience paid off.

Research and development for finding religious or spiritual groups

Using the phone book

The Yellow Pages list subject headings such as: religious organizations, churches, or synagogues.

The White Pages are helpful if you know the name of the religious facility.

Newspapers

Churches, Synagogues and the like, advertise in the Sunday editions of the newspaper, which sometimes include other information, such as, events and activities within the place of worship.

The Internet

Search the Internet by typing in the words: religion or philosophy, along with the name of your city or county. So your search would read: "Unitarian" "Des Moines."

Two popular religious singles' Internet addresses:

1. *Single Christian Network* at www.singlec.com

2. *Jewish Singles Connection* at, http://www.thejewish people.org/jsc/groupsplus.html

Also try http://www. switchboard.com, or http://

www.four11.com. Internet "phone books" in which you may look up churches, religious organizations, or synagogues.

__Networking__

Ask friends where they go to church. Find out if their church has an active singles' group.

Some phone numbers for singles religious groups across the country:

Westport Singles
C/o Unitarian Church
Westport, CT
(203) 227-1537

American Conf. of Sep. and Div. Catholics
Rochester, NY
(716) 271-1320

Timber-Lee Christian Singles
Troy, WI
(414) 642-7345

Natnl. Assoc. of Christian Singles Conf.
Milwaukee, WI
(414) 344-7300

Saddleback Community Church
Lake Forest, CA
(949) 581-5683

Coast Hills Community Church
Aliso Viejo, CA
(949) 362-0079

Westchester Singles
Unitarian Fellowship
Mt. Kisco, NY
(914) 245-1143

***

There's a singles Christian "hotline" for upcoming events in Orange County, California, that range from: retreats, progressive dinners, seminars, to dances, and a dating service. The phone number: (714) 375-0400.

Also, in The O.C. Times, I recently read of a new group called *405 Jewish Singles*. For information call Rabbi Gary Davidson at (562) 426-6413. This group targets Jewish men and women between the ages of 22-45.

Get Personal. . .Dating services and matchmakers

Therapeutic attitudes

Just another avenue

Some people have a negative opinion of those who use dating services or hire matchmakers. However, the persons utilizing these services are most often upstanding citizens. Many hold occupations requiring extensive work hours and haven't the time nor the energy to circulate. In other cases, there are a few who feel uncomfortable in large social settings, where the possibility of securing a date is greatest. A dating service or matchmaker becomes an avenue to meet people, where one feels more composure.

Others may link up with a dating service or matchmaker because it's simply another way to increase the odds of finding a mate. They may have tapped out introductions through friends, or exhausted other means of meeting available people.

An increasing number are back in the dating world again after a long period of time, due to a divorce, relationship breakups, or are new to the area. Most feel both apprehensive and clueless about reconnecting and establishing themselves in the dating world once more.

Perhaps when you hear the word "matchmaker" Fiddler on the Roof comes to mind. Back then, matchmakers were in such a business because matching corresponding wants and needs and, having many connections with others was their talent. It hasn't changed all that much today. Having a slew of contacts is one of the keys to a good matchmaker, and a large membership at a dating service will increase your odds for meeting your match.

Prescription for where to go

Dating Services and Matchmakers

Differences between dating services and matchmakers:
- Dating services allow you to select your own dates by the profiles and photographs provided by the clientele.

- Matchmakers choose the dates for you based on their knowledge of your preferences, personality and lifestyle, as compared with their clients' descriptions.

Cures for what to do

Ask the following questions to evaluate a dating or matchmaking service before joining:
- How many members belong?
- What's the age range?

- Do you screen people?
- Do you have any background requirements such as, educational or financial?
- Do you ask for personal or business references?
- What's the cost?
- What's the geographical proximity of your clientele?
- How long have you been in business?
- Do you have any guarantees?

Spending your hard-earned money on a service that's unable to provide numerable chances for meeting a mate is ludicrous. Some services will allow you to spend an evening at an introduction party or to attend a social event, where you may meet some of the members prior to joining. Certain dating services have reasonable rates and some matchmakers guarantee your membership until they've found your companion.

Services that allow you to know the workings of the establishment and possibly arrange for you to meet some clientele are best. If however, you sense either the people or their policies aren't quite right, don't join. Follow your intuition.

Theresa, a nurse at work, told me she should have followed her instincts when she joined an athletic/dating club. The owner seemed to have a boorish attitude and Theresa had an initial uneasy feeling about him, but the events sounded so engaging that she joined anyway. As it turned out, regular members of the club were of similar character. They all seemed to focus on the drinking parties afterwards, rather than on the recreational activities and games.

First-aid procedures for breaking the ice

The matchmaker or the dating service provide the information you need, so breaking the ice should be quite obvious. Speak of things you have in common by asking questions. Watch Charlie Rose, Jay Leno, Oprah Winfrey, or many of the other television personalities who interview others. Listen to their inquiries. They ask questions in a way that invites others to talk about themselves or situations in a nonthreatening manner.

I don't know about you, but I've been on dates where I felt grilled—as if I were on a job interview. A mere overview of hobbies and interests is all you want to know in the beginning, avoid prying or getting too personal. Finding out if the two of you are compatible by having a good time together is the first line of order.

Remedies and tips

Meeting for a drink at a coffeehouse or even breakfast at a coffee shop, is a quick way to meet without committing lots of time or money. Limit your efforts when meeting someone for the first time. If you find you're attracted to one another, it's then you'd consider spending more time and/or money.

Resource

Reaching any goal, be it a business, creative, or personal endeavor, may deplete your energy and drain you of an uplifting spirit. Especially when your goal takes time, tolerance, and patience; as finding a companion does. To keep your hopes up, with continued encouragement, listen to motivational tapes such as *See You at The Top* by Zig Ziglar. His talks are interesting because of the manner in which he tells his anecdotal stories; he can bring you to laughter and to tears—telling awesome stories of love, compassion, loyalty, and courage. He has a true talent to inspire us all.

Case study

Pixie, a friend who's a marriage and family counselor, told me about a client named Sheryl. Sheryl had about decided to quit dating because she'd been trying to meet a special person for a couple of years and it just wasn't happening.

With a last ditch effort she exhaustedly, and cynically, joined a dating service. Sheryl didn't think it was going to work, but had determined—dating service, or give up. As fate would have it, during the first week of joining, she received a postcard in the mail, stating—*Don, number 103, would like to meet you.* Don picked her from the photo book of over 350 women.

She proceeded to the office to look for Don, number 103, in the photograph album. She found him attractive and mailed a postcard back stating that *yes*, she, *number 221, would meet with him.*

An attraction for one another instantly followed. They started dating, and the frequency of their dates increased from—two times a week, to three and four times a week—until eventually they married.

Her name wasn't Cinderella: she was simply number 221. So, if it can happen for her, it can happen for you too.

Research and development for finding dating services and matchmakers

The Internet

Search the Web for a dating service in your area by typing in "dating services" or "matchmakers" and your "city" or "county." Placing quotation marks around the key words of your search makes the exploration more specific.

Some Internet addresses:

- *www.cupidnet.com/* Cupid Net is especially geared toward college singles for personal dating ads and matchmaking.
- *www.date.com/* Date Com. has personal dating ads.
- *www.singlescenter.com/index.htm* Singles Center is a compilation of many types of services, which include matchmaking and dating ads.
- *www.tableforsix.com.* Table for Six is a group where dinner parties for singles are arranged.
- *www.meetingforgood.com.* Meeting for Good is where singles unite and perform community work for a good cause.

***

A Mutual Friend is an Internet site with a different twist on dating. A Mutual Friend describes themselves as a finding service with people you've seen before. They help you to determine whether someone you already know, is interested in you.

Participants complete an expression of interest card, to be registered into a database. Your designated person will not be informed of your interest unless he or she registers an expression of interest in you. In that case, A Mutual Friend will tell you both through e-mail.

To increase your odds of meeting someone you're attracted to. Make the person aware of the service by slipping a piece of paper with the Web site address on to their desk, under the door, or by sending the address via e-mail through a friend.

The address is *www.amutualfriend.com/*. The e-mail address: amfriend@accessone.com.

The mailing address:
A Mutual Friend
218 Main Street #432
Kirkland, WA 98033
(452) 576-8411

Don't forget to use Datesmart on the Internet. The service that provides background checks on people you're interested in dating as previously mentioned in the chapter entitled Get High-tech.

Newspapers

Dating services or matchmakers can be found in most newspapers in the Thursday or Friday editions, either in the ads, or under places to go for singles, usually in the entertainment section.

Magazines

Dating services in singles and some regional magazines have listings in the advertisement sections. Refer to Treatment Plan Eleven for the names and addresses of singles magazines formerly mentioned.

Utilize the Phone Book

The Yellow Pages list by subject, look under dating services.

The White Pages list the proper name of the business.

Religious Organizations

Oftentimes larger churches or synagogues will have dating services. Try calling one of the larger churches or synagogues in your area. Or refer to Treatment Plan Fourteen in the research and development section, to find dating services through religious or spiritual organizations.

Great Expectations

This is one of the oldest and largest dating services nationwide. A few of the phone numbers around the country are:

Boston (617) 332-7755
Chicago (312) 943-1760
Denver (303) 321-151
Las Vegas (702) 734-6000
Los Angeles (310) 477-5566
Orange County (714) 476-1986

St. Louis (314) 291-6789

Washington DC (703) 847-0808

Call one of the numbers for the location nearest you or reach them on the Web at: http://www.great-expectations.com

Get Excited. . .Nightclubs, restaurants, and bars

Therapeutic attitudes

Are we having fun yet?

Many singles lament finding a date by barhopping. What baffles me, is that after interviewing many people, I've learned that the majority of them had met their husbands or wives in a bar. When they say bar, they usually don't mean "an alcoholic watering hole," but rather, they met their loved one in a restaurant that has a bar or lounge in it, where they do things other than drink, such as: play pool, dance, sing, or watch sports on television. Simply a way to have fun with others at night.

It isn't necessary to order an alcoholic beverage when in a bar or nightclub. You may prefer to choose sparkling water or soft drinks—popular and acceptable beverages.

Nightclubs often have the connotation of a "meat market." A meat market implies you're selected by your appearance, and if you aren't relatively handsome or beautiful, you don't get picked; but this isn't always true. How many times have you seen a good-looking man or a gorgeous woman, alone, because they appear aloof or apathetic? Whereas a person not quite as attractive; but more down to earth; is surrounded by others; having a fabulous time. Personality and openness are what attract others, even more than physical beauty.

Another one of the drawbacks of night clubbing, where the social unacceptability comes in to play, is in the abuse of alcohol. When people have had a few too many drinks they become obnoxious, insincere, or dishonest. Some don't have the courage to meet people or dance without a chemical dependency for sociability, which may be either a lifestyle or disease. It's likely you'll avoid coming across this problem if you both arrive and leave early. By getting there before nine in the evening and departing by eleven, you'll probably meet people who are there specifically to dance or play a game, such as darts or billiards.

Activities as dancing, or karaoke usually begin around nine, and heavy drinkers don't arrive until after eleven. Give yourself that two-hour window to have fun, and possibly meet someone. If you haven't met anybody by then, call it a night.

Dancing at a nightclub is a great way to get exercise. Singing on stage is an excellent way to conquer stage fright or hone up on performing skills. Playing pool is a good way of focusing your thoughts, and releasing the tensions of the day. Think of a nightclub as a place to improve your talents, or to release pent-up energy, while enjoying others and possibly connecting with a great guy or gal.

Prescription for where to go

Nightclubs, restaurants, and bars

These include:
- Cocktail Lounges
- Comedy Clubs
- Dance Clubs
- Game Rooms
- Karaoke Bars
- Pool or Billiard Rooms
- Restaurants
- Sports Bars

Cures for what to Do

Pick a club that's right for your interests and personality. Choose one with single people in your age range, where there's more to do than drink alcohol; one that has singing, dancing, comedy, or games.

To locate a nightclub suited to your preferences, call the manager or owner of the club and ask about their clientele and activities. Talk to some of the waiters or waitresses regarding entertainment, recreation, and ages of the patrons. Ask those who frequent clubs, where they go. Become willing to experiment in finding a club you like.

By becoming a regular at your favorite nightspot; going routinely; on the same night; at the same time each week, you'll see familiar faces and they'll recognize you. It's an efficient way to make friends and/or acquaintances and in turn get dates.

For Men

Ask women to dance whether you've been turned down in the past or not. Expect rejection and don't take it personally. Just as in sales, you should expect rejection nine times before you get a yes. The more times someone says no, the closer you are to that yes. Besides, I seriously doubt you'll be turned down that many times.

I'll share a secret with you about women: they want men to approach—they want men to pursue. I can't tell you how many women have left a dance early, or departed frustrated, because so many of the men didn't have the courage to ask them to dance.

For Women

A certain man may be summoning up the courage to ask you to dance, but notices how frequently you turn other men down. That discourages him from approaching, and if you were hoping to dance with that certain man, the chances have now become slim to none that he'll ask you. Dance for fun and exercise. Be open to dancing with all kinds of people. On the other hand, you don't have to accept slow dances with strangers. Be honest, but polite when you need to turn someone down.

* * *

Patricia, a curvy Irish, blonde told me of a time at a singles dance where short men asked her to slow dance. Her curves jutting to just the right spot for men of such stature. She turned them down, by saying, "I won't dance

184

to the slow tunes, but ask me again when there's a fast song."

First-aid procedures for breaking the ice

Here's a contrived, yet creative way to invite people out. You aren't really asking them for a date, but you'll clearly be making it easier for them to do so. Have one or more friends agree to meet at a club or restaurant on a certain night of the week, at the same time each week. Then, when you meet someone you'd like to know better, you can matter-of-factly invite him or her to join you and your friends to your "whatever night meeting spot." Creating an on-going gathering place is a good foundation for inviting people you come across in daily interactions, for a casual get together.

Choose a certain hour or two, on a specific night of the week, and invite someone with whom you're attracted, to come along. It could be someone you see often, or someone you just met. Ask him or her to drop by for a Coke, around that chosen time. Keep at it. If they don't show up the first time, invite them again. Persistence is a powerful tool for getting what we want, as long one is aware of understanding the fine line between tenacity and obstinacy.

How many times have you found yourself in a situation where you were attracted to someone during a fleeting encounter, wanting to continue a dialogue but didn't know what to do to get them to stay? So off into the sunset you both departed . . . never to meet again.

The following is an example of how a prearranged spot

helps in possibly becoming involved with people you meet, especially if the contact were brief.

Michelle met a very likable, good-looking man the other day, while at work. He helped in directing her to a certain address, and was flirting with her. She said, "You've been so helpful, I'd like to reciprocate by inviting you to join a few friends and me to The Rhythm and Blues Cafe, Tuesday night. We dance, listen to music, talk, and laugh. Bring your wife or a friend if you'd like."

She was being cordial and exercised her competency at breaking through fear of talking to new people. Michelle is a living example of making life happen— not waiting for life to "throw her a bone."

Michelle said he never did show up, leading us to believe he wasn't available. Although, only a guess, there ought to be laws that all married men wear wedding bands, as most women do.

More first-aid procedures for breaking the ice

Once you've arrived at the club of your choice, tell yourself to compliment five people throughout the evening. Say such things as:

- "I like your tie." ("I've been looking for one like that for my brother for his birthday. Where did you get it?")
- "You're a pleasure to be around." ("We're going to the Much More Fun Club next week, why don't you join us?")
- "You're an excellent dancer. ("Where did you learn to dance?")
- "Your dress is pretty." (" You look good in red.")

- "You two make the cutest couple." ("You're a great dance team.")

It doesn't matter whom you compliment, men or women; the point is to become involved with those around you and focus outward, rather than inward.

Case studies

Cindy, a pharmaceutical sales representative, made friends with John at a restaurant/bar one night. She'd gone out with a few girlfriends, and was geared for fun. She glanced around the room to note any interesting faces. She spotted a well-dressed man who had a pleasant, friendly appearance. Cindy sensed he'd be fun to talk to and approached him by saying, "I wish there were some men with pierced nostrils and tattoos around here. I guess I'll have to tolerate this conservatism for one night." John laughed and, to that he added, "I come because there's free food. I live out in my car and take showers at the gym. Why should I spend money on food or rent when I can live like this?"

They kept up a whimsical dialogue for awhile and had a great time. She excused herself, chatted with her girlfriends a bit longer, then drove home.

The following Wednesday, at the same restaurant and bar, John approached Cindy and asked if she'd be interested in going to another spot where he and his friend sang Karaoke. She said, "Sure." They told her about their usual Wednesday night routine: The Chanteclair, a French restaurant for wine tasting and hors d'oeuvres; then to Benihana's, a Japanese restaurant for Karaoke; and lastly, to The Atrium Hotel, for dancing to rock and roll music.

Cindy discovered she loved Karaoke, especially at Benihana's. People were there either to sing or to have dinner, unlike other places where she later found that were filled with people who needed to get drunk before they could conjure up the nerve to sing in front of a group.

John and his friend had graciously invited her into their Wednesday night world where she remained until the group slowly dispersed. The two men helped Cindy learn how to create her own fun, and to develop her own social circle of friends by networking in such a manner.

***

Jerry met his present wife, Toni, at a restaurant/nightclub. He first asked Estelle to dance, but she turned him down. It didn't discourage him though, because he asked the girl next to her, Toni, to dance. Jerry asked Toni for her phone number and called her later for a date. They dated frequently and exclusively, which lead to their marriage and the birth of a sweet baby girl a few years later.

Research and development for finding a nightclub, restaurant, or bar

Newspapers

Check the entertainment or lifestyle section of the Thursday or Friday edition of the paper.

Local, free newspapers often list club locations. Regional restaurants, and/or bars, place advertisements.

Utilize the Phone Book

The Yellow Pages list subject headings. Look under cocktail lounges, nightclubs, restaurants, comedy clubs, or sports bars. Call to find out if they have dancing, Karaoke, darts, billiards, or other activities.

The White Pages list the club, bar, or restaurant by name.

Networking

Ask friends and acquaintances which places they frequent. Certain clubs cater to particular age ranges and other nights seem to attract more singles. Specific clubs and bars have varied activities.

Check places out

Next time you're driving by a restaurant, bar, or club, walk in and talk to the employees or the manager. Ask if they have a flyer or roster of events.

Bookstores

Check the regional section for books or guides to local restaurants and the like. Many regional and metropolitan magazines offer listings or recommendations for restaurants, nightclubs, or bars.

Get On With It. . .Summation and calendars

Therapeutic attitudes

Priorities

The past sixteen chapters have outlined different ways to target your dating market and various methods to forging ahead. Regardless the route you've decided to take, be assured that it requires time and effort and therefore, your desire to be with someone to love must be a high priority in your life. With a limited life span, it's important to know which activities hold the highest priority for you.

Some women may be in a hurry to find "Mr. Right" because their time clocks are running out. A youthful appearance is nature's way of magnetizing the opposite sex for reproduction purposes. Taking too casual an approach in finding a mate, or waiting for someone who's perfect, could end up being a costly mistake if you want children. You may wake up one day to find your chances of meeting available; quality people are slimmer and slimmer. The same goes for men wanting children— the sooner the better.

Yet, despite a person's age, our wants aren't much different. Most have the desire and need for companionship. Try to find someone you respect, with whom you have common interests and lifestyle preferences.

Remember to be young at heart, empathetic, and flexible. Be willing to do what it takes to get along as a couple, so that you may create a remarkable life for you and your partner-to-be.

Lose the new age attitude and get on with the new millennium

Who wants to be alone? One of the new age attitudes of the 90's has been based on the social premise that, "If you love yourself, then you're okay and you don't need anyone else to make you feel whole." Of course we need to love ourselves, but sharing our lives with another is what makes most people feel complete. It's a warm feeling to know you have someone to come home to; someone who cares and knows all about you; someone who'll love and support you through the good times and the bad.

Another of my favorite new age social sayings that I love to hate is, "I found my mate when I stopped looking." What I detest most about it is the phrasing. The person who found his or her mate really didn't stop looking; they just stopped placing so much energy on finding "the one." They simply no longer exuded energy of over- eagerness, which oftentimes scares people away.

The person who found their mate when they stopped looking, had most likely depleted their last resource for meeting a great guy or gal, and had given up on the idea for awhile. Then, they thought it to be a miracle when they met someone special! Deep down, they never gave up hope, nor did they stop having a social life. The natural desire for a companion remained. It's just one of the great cosmic jokes—the law of nature—that proves—when you stop pursuing something, it falls right into your lap.

Another perspective on the new age saying of, I found may mate when I stopped looking, follows: you've applied for lots of jobs and didn't get an interview, so gave up on the search. You did everything you could—yet nothing happened. Then a few days later, a colleague calls with an opportunity at his or her company and, what a miracle, you found a job! And you weren't even looking! You were, looking; it just didn't show up on the path you were searching.

We can't force ourselves to stop the innate desire for a partner. But by altering the energy we emanate; by keeping the faith; and holding on to hope; by leaving our worries and concerns with a higher force; we're able to have peace of mind; which creates a calm essence of being.

Besides, this is no longer a new age, it's a new millennium and the human desire to be with a companion will stay with us until eternity. If you want to be with someone, good for you, be thankful that you love enough to share yourself with another.

Follow your heart

Don't allow others to make you feel wrong about trying to find someone to love. I've had people tell me I was "desperate" and that I ought to relax and let life happen. I didn't feel desperate—exasperated maybe—but not desperate. It seems people who bestow such advice, are the ones who are married, tainted, or unhappy in their own relationships. Yet there's some accuracy to the perception of being desperate. Again, it follows one of the universal truths—the harder you try to make something happen, the further it eludes you.

In order to diminish this desperate stance, I've used the following prayer, "I give up God, I'm not in control, and you are. I don't know what you have in store for me, but I do know it's up to me to show up for social engagements and be the best person I can as I follow the golden rule. If it's your will, a special person will find me."

What you see is what you get

Be good to yourself. Deluding ourselves of the truth is an easy trap to fall into. If a man isn't ambitious, he's not going to change; if he hasn't any fashion sense, he'll not likely transform his image for you; if she has a controlling nature, she'll probably continue to control. Accept a man or woman as each is, or move on.

Applicably, if you're in a dismal relationship now, it makes no sense continue simply because you fear it would create despairing feelings of loneliness. The lonely feelings will pass, but recovering lost time won't.

Staying open-minded with a willingness to give is one of the secrets to maintaining valuable relationships. Adaptability will keep us young, until we're very, very old. At no time believe that you won't or can't adapt to living with another person. You have the power to change your mind and attitude to fulfill your love life. Love is invaluable. Do what it takes to find someone special. Don't allow fear to rule your life; in no way stop believing in love; and cease only when you've reached your goal. Good luck and God bless you.

The last and most important thing you need to know

Winston Churchill gave an oration to his freezing, bone-weary, British Troops during World War II, when the soldiers were desperate—contemplating defeat. The great Mr. Churchill, a man of such eloquence, gave a powerful speech by repeating a simple message for minutes on end. He told his loyal troops the following: "Never, never, give up."

Cures for what to do

Using the plan

Go back through the book to the activities you've highlighted. Read and reread the book for inspiration to stay on target with your goals. I know you'll meet the man or woman of your dreams by following the plan.

Blank calendars are provided. Refer to Chapter One for sample ways to schedule events.

Fill out your social calendar at the beginning of each month. Write an event in for each day, even if you aren't sure you'll go. The point is to have something to do everyday of the week if you want. You'll never be stranded without anywhere to go when a pang of unexpected loneliness strikes or when you have extra time on your hands. You'll know what to do, because you've written it down.

Sun.	Mon.	Tues.	Wed.	Thur.	Fri.	Sat.

Sun.	Mon.	Tues.	Wed.	Thur.	Fri.	Sat.

Sun.	Mon.	Tues.	Wed.	Thur.	Fri.	Sat.

Sun.	Mon.	Tues.	Wed.	Thur.	Fri.	Sat.

Sun.	Mon.	Tues.	Wed.	Thur.	Fri.	Sat.

Sun.	Mon.	Tues.	Wed.	Thur.	Fri.	Sat.

Sun.	Mon.	Tues.	Wed.	Thur.	Fri.	Sat.

Sun.	Mon.	Tues.	Wed.	Thur.	Fri.	Sat.

Sun.	Mon.	Tues.	Wed.	Thur.	Fri.	Sat.

About the Author

Gail Burgess has compiled workable steps for those who prefer not to be single. Her experience is based on many years of staying active and dating frequently. She has been a marketing and public relations' representative and fundraiser; the basic foundation for her grasp on the methods needed to socialize and meet others with ease.

Gail has had articles published in many medical newsletters, in addition to *The Easy Reader Newspaper* and *The San Gabriel Valley Magazine*.

Being a registered nurse, she carries a medical theme throughout the text, making it fun and easy to follow, as the reader learns to open his or her eyes, ears, and heart to let love in.

Gail has performed as a stand-up comic with an appearance on *The Joe Crummy Show* at KFI talk radio in Los Angeles. This background, along with acting as master of ceremonies at events, a speaker for many groups, along with a recent television commercial, brings a charisma to this engaging and essential book for those who are truly serious about dating and meeting someone to love.

Gail Burgess graduated for the University of New York with a degree in nursing and is a Registered Nurse. She lives in California.

*For the money-back guarantee, mail a copy of your receipt, a copy of your calendar, the reason you didn't get a date, and the book, and Social Lite Productions will gladly refund your money.

Instant Dating Starter Kit

You get . . .

- Pre-written ads . . . all you have to do is personalize them
- How to look your best on a date by knowing what to wear
- The five secrets men should know about women
- The five secrets women should know about men
- How to show someone a good time on a shoestring

Please send me the instant dating starter kit.

Name: _______________________________________

Address: _____________________________________

____

Phone number: ________________________________

Send $3.00 for shipping and handling to:

Social Lite Productions
31441 Santa Margarita Pkwy, PMB A359
Rancho Santa Margarita, CA 92688